REASON AND THE PASSIONS

PURDUE UNIVERSITY MONOGRAPHS
IN ROMANCE LANGUAGES

Volume 11

David Jonathan Hildner

Reason and the Passions
in the 'Comedias' of Calderón

DAVID JONATHAN HILDNER

REASON AND THE PASSIONS

IN THE *COMEDIAS* OF CALDERÓN

JOHN BENJAMINS PUBLISHING COMPANY
Amsterdam/Philadelphia

1982

To my wife Bertha

for her love and support

Table of Contents

Acknowledgments

I would like to express my especial thanks to Dr. Nicholas Spadaccini of the University of Minnesota, who directed this work in its original form as a doctoral dissertation. His guidance and friendship all through my student years have proved invaluable. Thanks are also due to Drs. Anthony Zahareas and Wlad Godzich, who served as readers on my dissertation committee, and to the editorial board of PUMRL for their help in revising the manuscript.

Finally, thanks are due to Dr. Benito Brancaforte, who was kind enough to read the manuscript and to offer valuable suggestions.

Note on the Texts

I have quoted on several occasions from the following plays by Calderón: *El médico de su honra,* in *Dramas de honor,* ed. Angel Valbuena Briones, 3rd ed., II (Madrid: Espasa-Calpe, 1970), 1-118; *El mayor monstro los çelos,* ed. Everett W. Hesse (Madison: University of Wisconsin Press, 1955); *A secreto agravio, secreta venganza,* in *Dramas de honor,* ed. Angel Valbuena Briones, I (Madrid: Espasa-Calpe, 1967), 1-96; *La gran Cenobia,* in *Primera parte de comedias,* ed. Angel Valbuena Briones (Madrid: Consejo Superior de Investigaciones Científicas, 1974), I, 1-85; *Los cabellos de Absalón,* ed. Gwynne Edwards (Oxford: Pergamon Press, 1973); *En la vida todo es verdad y todo mentira,* ed. Don William Cruickshank (London: Tamesis, 1971); *La estatua de Prometeo,* ed. Charles V. Aubrun (Paris: Centre de Recherches de l'Institut d'Etudes Hispaniques, 1965); *El mágico prodigioso,* in *Comedias religiosas,* ed. Angel Valbuena Briones, 3rd ed. (Madrid: Espasa-Calpe, 1946), I, 119-230; *Las cadenas del demonio,* in *Obras completas,* 5th ed. (Madrid: Aguilar, 1969), I, 643-74. Readers will be aware of the fact that there is no consistent modernization of spelling. I have followed in each case the edition indicated rather than attempt modernizing the texts or using the less reliable Aguilar *Obras completas,* which has modernized all spelling.

Introduction

In 1675, six years before the death of Calderón, Benedict de Spinoza began to circulate cautiously among his friends and colleagues in the Netherlands the manuscripts of what was to be published posthumously as the *Ethics*. Two of the principal building blocks of his system are found in the following definitions of good and evil: "By good, I understand that which we certainly know to be useful to us. By evil, on the contrary, I understand that which we certainly know hinders us from possessing anything that is good" (Part IV, Defs. 1-2). Spinoza's stand is naturalistic and pragmatic.

Calderón's education, on the other hand, carried out in Madrid's Colegio Imperial and in Salamanca, was replete with theological discoursing on the spiritual, invisible *summum bonum,* God, toward whom all right human action was to be directed. God's attributes and his mode of intervention in human affairs were definable in terms of Aristotelian and patristic thought, and thus the nature and proper activity of man, who was God's image and likeness, could be derived from the divine nature. The finite could only be ordered with a view toward the infinite, and the imperfect "here" had to look to the perfect "there" for guidance and salvation. This perfect being, however, was considered to be radically distinct from man, so that man's path to his preordained *summum bonum* led through many activities and states which were not "useful" in the sense in which Spinoza uses this word. It meant, at least in theory, the subordination of natural desires to a supernatural goal in the *patria* (Heaven), the renunciation of sensorial goods for the supernatural benefits of the next life.

While Calderón's *autos* portray this teleological view of life with unequaled ingenuity (for he is skillful in embodying abstract concepts in visible forms), his *comedias* lie somewhere on the line of development of European thought and activity between the other-worldiness of orthodox Thomism and the naturalism of which Spinoza's ideas are one example among many. Let us characterize the *comedias* briefly by stating that the motives which move the dramatic action forward are generally of a teleological nature; that is, they envisage some hypostatized end outside the individual characters. Yet, there are key moments when it becomes apparent to the reader or spectator that these ends have been created and set before the characters by themselves, by the requirements of their social standing in the play, by the manipulating dramatist Calderón,[1] or, in broader terms, by the social climate of the audience for whom these plays were written and performed. This countertendency in Calderón's *comedias* receives a later philosophical expression in another statement from Spinoza's *Ethics*: "[I]t is plain, therefore, that we neither strive for, wish, seek nor desire anything because we think it to be good, but, on the contrary, we adjudge a thing to be good because we strive for, wish, seek or desire it" (Part III, Prop. IX, Scholium). Such a statement was meant to remove man from the realm of final causes into the natural scientific realm of efficient causes, which in Spinoza's system form an uninterrupted and infinite chain of forces which determine the behavior of both natural bodies and human beings.

In this study we will examine to what extent this sort of naturalistic thinking is present in Calderón's *comedias* and whether it makes any dent in what has been recognized by most critics of the last fifty years as "Calderón's world view."

However, if we merely place Calderón's "thought" on a philosophic scale between medieval and Enlightenment thought, our study will suffer from an abstractness which is the curse of much speculation on Calderón's world view. He is called in various studies a "Catholic writer," a "Thomist," a "Counter-Reformation dramatist." His Augustinian, classical, Stoic, and other antecedents have been pointed out. Critical studies then try to put together a fairly consistent *Weltanschauung* for the dramatist. It becomes a question of showing how the "themes" or "theses" of the various groups of *comedias* fit into the world view, a task which often requires Herculean efforts.

Calderón's Christianity is the focal point around which revolve the major descriptions of his world view. This generalization provides a handle by which to grasp many aspects of his work. His Catholicism has been brought forward by some as an unavoidable limitation of his age and nation which prevented him from equaling the more secular dramatic successes of Shakespeare and Racine. It is used by others to exalt him as un upholder of the "true" values of primitive or pure Christianity against the "false" values of his society, such as honor, ambition, and ecclesiastical formalism.[2] Under many of these interpretations, however, lies an uncritical use of the word "Christian" and even of the more precise term "Counter-Reformation." Occasionally an important fact has been neglected: that, although the theology and philosophy which Calderón absorbed in his education may have been verbally identical with the major texts of St. Thomas and his followers, those ideas and terms were affirmed in Hapsburg Spain under radically different conditions from those under which St. Thomas wrote in the thirteenth century.[3] It is ahistorical to assume that the transmission of a set of dogmas over three and a half centuries could have resulted in an identical attitude toward these dogmas or that the function of any Scholastic concept in its social context could be the same in one century as in another. It may be that Calderón, by his conscious use of Scholastic terminology, was attempting to revive the more organic and coherent quality of original Thomism. Yet, a close look at the dramatic texts of his *comedias* reveals anything but a pure Scholasticism. The changes in the structure of imperial Spanish society could not but influence Calderón's thought patterns. To read his texts with these changes in mind leads the reader to examine carefully the dramatic context in which the central concepts of reason and passions are treated.

Many modern editions of the *comedias* tend to cite passages from St. Thomas in order to elucidate key Calderonian concepts such as *discreción* and *prudencia*. Calderón is presented as having recaptured a Christian wholeness like that of the high Middle Ages in his own time. Yet it is often forgotten that other writers, such as Gracián and Quevedo, exhibit a fragmentation and disillusionment which are unmistakably Baroque.[4] A. A. Parker, for example, finds an enlightened Catholic "conceptual clarity" in Calderón which deepens and humanizes his dramatic vision of life and which elevates him above the "false" values which obsessed his society. In some cases the desire to see such tendencies in Calderón becomes "a kind of critical wishful thinking."[5]

In view of these difficulties of interpreting Scholasticism within Calderón's works, I will attempt to implement the following methodological rule in this study: the use of Scholastic terms, concepts, or methods of disputation in Calderón must not lead us to suppose that the key to our interpretation lies necessarily in the relevant passages from the *Summa Theologiae* or even from sixteenth- or seventeenth-century Spanish *summas* or treatises derived from St. Thomas. Those texts will serve to point out what Calderón's dramatic world is and what it is not. Through an uncritical use of these texts, we would be tacitly acquiescing in the acceptance of the "angelic doctor's" teaching as an enduring body of doctrine which guides the philosophical and peda-gogical practice of the Catholic Church and, by extension, of all men. This is what Parker means when he speaks of Calderón's deeply "human" view. Such an assumption puts Calderón into the role of one more in a series of explicators and transmitters of a timeless truth.

The obvious success of this exegetical approach in clarifying the content of the *autos* has led to the establishment of these sacramental plays as an exegetical canon to be used as a reference grid for orienting critical work on the *comedias*.[6] A system for a Calderonian hermeneutics is thus established and the development of criticism on these plays consists in the full exploita-tion of this arsenal of Scholastic concepts in interpreting the individual works.[7] In order to save the reference framework from harm, emphasis is placed on the unity and coherence of medieval thought. If conflicting Scho-lastic schools are admitted into the picture, an attempt is made to establish to which of these schools Calderón adhered. At times, critics attribute to Calderón an eclecticism which becomes fruitless because it does not attempt to state what *was* the organizing principle of his selection of sources and materials. These are, in general and abstract form, some of the difficulties that have been encountered by modern critics in the determination of Calderón's world view.

When a history of ideas is applied to his works, it is categorically assumed that Counter-Reformation Spain was dominated by "Catholic orthodoxy," a concept which is dealt with as a monolithic block.[8] Very little criticism on Calderón contains even the dialectical element of an idealist *Geistesgeschichte,* in which ideas have a history which is fundamentally transformed over time.[9] For Neo-Thomist critics of a "Thomistic" writer, Calderón's dramaturgy is just as applicable to life in the twentieth century as to medieval and Baroque times.[10] However, a dialectical thinker, even though he may move solely in the sphere of intellectual and artistic production, realizes that there is no such thing as undifferentiated static duration of ideas. Their establishment immediately produces an inner division (Hegel's *Scheidung in sich*) which breaks the wholeness of the original concept and forces it to move. The Calderonian metaphor of the serpent which begets children that devour their progenitor, a metaphor which in orthodox Christian thought is applied only to the evil man, becomes a universal metaphor in dialectical thinking and comes to signify the inevitable forward movement of human thought itself. In short, when we use medieval ideas to explicate Calderón, let us allow them the full conflictiveness which they contain. Let us give the Devil his due, even in the works of a dramatist who was so firmly opposed to the Devil and all his works.[11]

Rather than concentrate on the content of medieval concepts which are "embodied" in Calderón's secular works, we should direct our attention to his methods of representation. If we analyze the Latin noun *repraesentatio,* we extract the root *praesens,* "present." Since Calderonian characters remark that all of life is *representaciones,* then *a fortiori* we can say the same about the *comedias* themselves. In reference to our theme of reason and the passions, the problem assumes the following guise: the mental movements of intellect, imagination, memory, and rational will are not themselves sensorial, although they can operate on sensorial objects. If, then, they are to be expressed on the stage, they must be represented. Passions and thoughts occur within a subject, but for the outward observer these movements are not present unless they are *made* present to him by visible or audible signs.

Another way of expressing the same duality is to distinguish between private and public occurrences. The phenomena which Aristotle and St. Thomas described as taking place within the soul are private. These philosophers gained philosophical knowledge about these phenomena either through introspection or by speculating about what must take place in the mind, given the natures of God and man. When the mental movements become bodily movements, locomotion, movements of the limbs, facial expressions, or articulated speech, we move into the realm of public occurrences. All of the occurrences on Calderón's stage are public, a fact which critics tend to overlook. W. J. Entwistle, for example, in an article on the temptation of Justina, treats the heroine as a real life subject and takes at face value the words used by her and the Devil to describe her state of mind.[12] To the case study information gathered from the play, Entwistle proceeds to apply Thomistic doctrine on reason, passions, and demonic temptation. This kind of study disregards another primary methodological requisite: to keep in mind that Calderonian characters, even when speaking in asides or monologues, are not alone, since they are always speaking in the presence of an audience. It is evident from Calderón's style that he never forgot this principle. As further evidence we can mention the abundance of rhetorical structures inherent in Calderonian discourse and remind ourselves that rhetoric is the art of *public* speaking.

An examination of the monologues of the "husbands of honor" in Chapter 2 will show that Calderonian protagonists have a listener at all times, even if it be the character himself. Benedetto Croce has placed a negative valuation on this trait of Calderón's style: "E uno stile di chi sa di avere dinanzi un ascoltatore da informare, da scuotere, da intrattenere, un ascoltatore a cui [Semíramis] fornisce un' analisi di sé stessa, innanzi a lui giocando di virtuosità."[13] This judgement reflects Croce's fundamental distinction between rhetoric and poetry. The former is for him a practical activity associated with persuasion, teaching, and impressing an audience, while the latter is an expressive activity which exteriorizes inner feelings and imaginative states.

We find a similar distinction made in the linguistic thought of Roman Jakobson, who speaks of the expressive function of language, in which attention is centered on the sender of the linguistic message, the conative function, where an attempt is made to produce an effect upon the receiver of the message, and the poetic function, in which attention is centered on the message itself. The poetic function can, of course, serve the expressive and conative functions and there is no reason to suppose that it cannot serve both at once. We know that in Calderón's age no such distinction between poetry and rhetoric was consistently formulated; poetics grew out of oratorical rhetoric. Thus John V. Bryans, although he makes a distinction between "passionate speeches" and "persuasive speeches," admits that the two cannot be rigidly separated.[14] In Calderón's *comedias* the relation sender-receiver can take on various forms. There are soliloquies and asides, in which we can assume either that the sender and receiver are the same person or that the audience is meant to be the receiver. We find apostrophes, in which the receiver is not the same person as the sender, but a fiction brought forth by the sender's imagination. Likewise, Calderón includes long monologues spoken by one character to another character onstage. Given this shifting relationship, it is not easy to determine whether a speech is primarily expressive or conative, whether, to return to Croce's terminology, it belongs to lyricism or oratory. The problem is complicated by the fact that each *comedia* can be considered to be one long written message sent by Calderón to his readers.

It is important to remember in this regard that Calderonian characters always hear themselves speak. Otherwise there would be no justification for the frequent self-interruption and self-correction which they practice through such expressions as "¿Qué digo?", "Mal dije," and others. So even in monologues spoken in the presence of another character, the speaker is also a listener, that is, a receiver of the message. A primarily conative or oratorical speech will then have the effect of producing emotion not only in the other character but also in the speaker himself. Ironically, Calderón often has the listening character react in an indifferent or unexpected manner and has him carry out his intentions exactly as he planned before hearing the speech, while the speaker reaches a high pitch of emotion and is dramatically changed by the experience of delivering the monologue.

In Act III of *El príncipe constante,* Fernando pleads with the King of Fez in a speech which is some 169 verses long, but the king continues in his inflexible attitude and refuses to grant the Portuguese prince a release from suffering either through physical remedies or a swift death. On the other hand, within Fernando's monologue the whole dramatic action of the play takes a step forward, for it is there that Fernando speaks directly for the first time of an active desire to die for the Catholic faith, not wherever Providence decides, but in the captivity of Fez; this is more than just a patient Stoic *constancia* such as he had shown in the first two acts. In other words, this monologue represents his first attempt to act in hastening his inevitable death. It is important to note that from the moment he is carried onstage by his friends until the moment he begins his plea by kissing the Moorish king's foot, he does not say anything, either in an aside or to another character, that would indicate an intention to ask the king for death. In fact, just before his speech, he asks the passers-by in the street to give him alms to sustain *life,* just like any Spanish or Moslem beggar: " ¡Oh, si pudiera / mover a alguno a piedad / mi voz, para que siquiera / un instante más viviera / padeciendo!"[15]

Thus a problem arises as to the point in the action at which the intention to ask for death comes into being in Fernando's mind. Given the verses just quoted, it is possible to assume that it occurs during the speech, most likely during his general observations on human life and death. In any case, the determination of the turning point is not essential to our purpose here; one need only state the problem to realize that neither of the terms "oratory" and "lyric expression" adequately characterizes the nature of the monologue in question. It is neither simply the outpouring of a passion heretofore hidden in his breast nor just a calculated plea to obtain a favor from the king. Pring-Mill is partially right when he says: "Para Calderón, diríase—a base de un estudio de su teatro–que todas las funciones del lenguaje como medio de comunicación pudieran reducirse a las dos artes hermanadas de la Lógica (para razonar) y la Retórica, empleada ésta para persuadir y conmover *y por lo tanto para expresar las emociones.*"[16] The expression of emotions often does arise from the attempt to persuade and teach. Yet the converse also contains a grain of truth: the attempt to persuade is fed by the emotions. In Bryans' treatment of Calderón's "passionate manner," his theory of the function of rhetoric is not fully developed enough to correct the misleading impression that the characters experience preexisting emotions or reactions to a situation in their minds, which they then proceed to express through rhetorical tropes and figures.[17]

Unlike Calderón's protagonists, a political orator (especially a disciple of Machiavelli) must keep in mind certain calculated actions and effects that he wishes to produce in his audience, and he uses all the instruments of oratorical rhetoric to produce them. His strategy is lost if his objective changes in mid-speech. Likewise, a Scholastic debater sets out to prove, through logical argument, a preestablished intellectual thesis. Fernando and other dramatic characters are no such unmoved movers. Their process of reasoning evokes emotions, which in turn evoke desires and aversions. These movements of the will avail themselves of verbal artifice (both logical and rhetorical) to influence the behavior of others or the speaker's own behavior in the case of soliloquies. Thus Pring-Mill's expression *estructuras lógico-retóricas* should be amended to read *estructuras lógico-poético-retóricas.*

Let us return to Bryans' correct observation that it is often difficult to classify speeches in the *comedias* as persuasive or passionate. A deeper analysis of the reasons for this ambivalence will show that the problem is traceable in part to the inadequacies of the categories employed in the rhetorical treatises of antiquity and of the Renaissance. Rhetoric was said to have various aims, which varied from one author to another, among them (1) persuasion in public speeches, which for the original Greek rhetoricians was its only function, and (2) teaching, since not all truth could be presented to all persons in the same way. A conflict between these two aims is evident in Plato, who condemns the sophistic possibilities of persuading others to commit immoral acts or believe false statements. Thus Cicero says that the orator should come *non ex rhetorum officinis sed ex academiae spatiis,* "not from the workshops of the rhetoricians but from the halls of the academy." And Quintilian defines the ideal orator as a *vir bonus dicendi peritus,* "a morally good man who is expert in speaking."[18] Calderón's *comedias* are bursting with situations which illustrate this dilemma. To these two aims must be added (3) ornamentation of speech for the purpose of arousing pleasure or other emotions in the listener or reader. Just as the art of persuasion was counterpoised by moral restrictions, so excessive ornamentation was criticized by various doctrines of decorum, in other words, of that which is fitting for a certain situation (Aristotle *to prepon*). Such doctrines were designed to protect speech both against obscurity, with consequent loss of the literal meaning, and, in the Christian era, against the sensorially appealing embellishments that might distract the receiver of the message from a moral lesson. This is a concern which is voiced in Castilian literature as early as the *Libro de buen amor*. Counter-Reformation Spain inherits these problems in those terms which could be taken as almost a motto of its artistic program: *enseñar deleitando* and *deleitar enseñando*. But alongside these two skills of teaching and amusing appears another, which found very little place in traditional rhetorical theory: *representar*. It is to this end that the poetical procedures of the dramatic characters' speeches tend.

Thus, the Baroque dramatist makes no effort to conceal the fact that everything that happens in his plays is *representaciones*. Walter Benjamin speaks of "the display of the craftsmanship, which, in Calderón especially, shows through like the masonry in a building whose rendering has broken away."[19] If this study concerns itself mainly with the concrete words and actions of the *comedias,* this is not due to a refusal to look beyond the phenomena to abstract truths. Rather, it is due to the increasingly apparent fact that Calderón's secular dramaturgy envisages above all the manner in which a nonsensorial content is made visible and audible. Calderón seems so busy creating a massive presence of sounds and sights out of the absence of a silent, empty stage that the question as to whether this presence is a faithful re-presentation of inner thoughts and feelings becomes obscured.

As we take apart certain representative word patterns and metaphors, we will attempt to show that the keys to their interpretation are to be found not only in the realm of metaphysics and moral theology, as has been assumed in scores of Calderonian studies, but also in the civil and political relations in which Calderón and his audience were inextricably involved. The problem of reason and passions cannot be dealt with in abstract terms alone. Rather, it must be related to the idea and practice of *aristocratic* behavior. The etymological meaning of the term "aristocracy" is "rule of the best," which leads immediately into a dichotomy. Does the aristocracy rule because it is composed of the "best" people according to a preordained principle of reason, or is it composed of the "best" people because it is the class of rulers? We will exemplify this and other dichotomies in Chapters 2-5 by means of examples from the four major realms of human life portrayed by Calderón: the sanctity of honor in marriage, the art of statecraft, the problem of obtaining knowledge, and the phenomenon of religious conversion. This division is a traditional one based on the hierarchical priorities of human life as given by Scholastic theology and on a certain division of types of *comedias* which Calderón inherited from Lope de Vega. It will be seen that, in the *comedias* under consideration, these divisions interpenetrate one another.

Since reason and the passions, unlike certain other themes, cannot be dealt with in Calderón except through a more or less detailed analysis of behavior patterns of specific characters, my discussion in each chapter will be limited to two or three plays, with passing references to others. In this way, we may follow a train of thought or the progress of a passion through more than one scene. This procedure has seemed preferable to an accumulation of short examples from many plays. Other plays could have been substituted for those studied here, with perhaps slightly different results. Although the procedure used here does lay the writer open to objections based on plays or groups of plays not treated in this study, nevertheless this danger is smaller in the case of Calderón than in those of Shakespeare or Racine, or even that of Lope de Vega. Readers familiar with a large number of Calderón's *comedias* know that there is a sort of system of formulas in his secular works, some of whose characteristics are found in every play. A close examination of even one Calderonian *comedia* puts the reader well on the way to an acquaintance with many others. Thus, depth of analysis has taken precedence over breadth of exemplification, with the expectation that each reader will apply the notions developed here to the *comedias* with which he is most familiar.

In the matrimonial realm, *El médico de su honra* and *A secreto agravio secreta venganza* form a pair of very similar honor plays which allow us to examine the ratiocinations of dishonored husbands closely. This is not the case with Calderón's other important honor play, *El pintor de su deshonra*, which we will not treat in this study. Its protagonist does not go through the same complex process of rationalization of his act of revenge. I include *El mayor monstruo los celos* as a matrimonial play which has no overriding concern for honor and as one which begins to deal with imperial politics. Political dramas are represented by *La gran Cenobia,* which takes place in an ancient pagan kingdom, and *Los cabellos de Absalón,* which brings in the element of religion allied with statecraft. *En la vida todo es verdad y todo mentira* illustrates a multitude of Calderón's favorite philosophical themes, without obligating us to delve into the storms of controversy and literature that surround *La vida es sueño.* Except for the "rebel soldier" problem treated briefly in a later chapter, it seems that at each step in a study of *La vida es sueño* the critic must skirt or tackle difficult and often violent polemics which would distract us from the central theme, so that *En la vida,* which has many thematic and argumental similarities to it, seems better suited to the present purpose. *La estatua de Prometeo,* being a play about a thinker and inventor whose twin brother is a hunter, is perhaps the most appropriate of the mythological dramas, although any of these late plays and *zarzuelas* provides much material for our theme. Finally, among the *comedias de santos,* I have selected two extreme examples: *Las cadenas del demonio* depends heavily on crowd-pleasing miracles and stage machinery, while *El mágico prodigioso* tries to portray the inner processes of temptation and conversion on stage. The one well-known *comedia* that does not fit into any category is *El alcalde de Zalamea,* since it is the most "Lopesque" of all; that is, it owes most to Lope's relatively unreflective stage language. Thus the interplay of ratiocination and passion is not as highly developed as in his more characteristic plays and we will not deal with it.

It has been traditional to regard the problem of religious conversion, which borders on the subject matter of the *autos*, as the foundation of the other three realms. The religious dramas deal with eternal matters, which in Scholastic thought take precedence over temporal affairs. This study does not share the above presupposition. It is concerned rather with the methods of justification of aristocratic behavior in all four realms; both reason and exalted passions become the preserve of noble blood in Calderón's plays. Whether he is dealing with vengeful husbands, monarchs, usurpers, contemplative men of learning, or saints, the thread of social distinction never disappears. The concern of his characters that they not commit a *bajeza*, a "low" action, is not simply a Christian concern with avoiding sin, since Catholicism itself is rallied to the cause of aristocracy, whose noble blood is one of the *causas ministras* that God's providence uses in carrying out its designs.[20] The characters are much more concerned with practicing a virtue (*virtus*) which will distinguish them from the vulgar, since they are conscious that they are the *casos notables,* the exceptional people, who are performing exemplary actions on the stage of the world theater.[21] Whether these actions are examples to be imitated (e.g., the steadfast prince Fernando) or examples to be avoided (e.g., Semíramis and Herodes) is not the major issue in Calderón.

This is the matrix on which we must base our conception of reason and the passions. We will see that reason is not only the preordained principle by which these high-minded aristocrats exercise the functions that have been given to them but also the tool which they use to maintain themselves in an uppermost position. Passions are not only the negative impulses which the noble character must shun because they detract from his arduous endeavor but also the spiritual energy that lifts him above common human nature and makes him a *caso notable.* After our discussion of such cases in nine *comedias* of various types arranged in an ascending hierarchical order, we will try to determine whether the supremacy of "right reason" in the Thomistic sense adequately represents Calderón's presentation of this theme.

The Thomistic Scheme of Reason and the Passions

The Thomistic doctrine of the soul falls into two parts in accordance with the two ways in which the soul is related to the outside world.[1] In one order, things have an "entitative" existence, that is, an existence as entities in the real world. In Aristotle and most Scholastic treatises, the human faculties which deal with this type of object are called appetitive. All types of appetite strive to appropriate the object in its external existence. There is real motion or tendency of the spirit toward that which it is not. In another order, things can be said to have an "intentional" existence insofar as they are known, in the fact that they are present in a knowing subject. The faculties which apprehend their objects in this mode are called cognitive. Since the objects of the soul's faculties range from material objects to spiritual beings, there is a corresponding range of cognitive and appetitive faculties.

This range of objects is not a horizontal one, showing different but equal portions of being. It is definitely a vertical one, which places certain realms of being as unequivocally higher than others. The criterion for placing objects in this hierarchy is their immateriality. Insofar as a being is nonmaterial, i.e., insofar as its form is freed from the necessary character of matter, it is said to be *in actu* or active, since it is moving itself and other beings rather than merely being acted upon. Such a being is also enabled to exercise freedom, both freedom from determinism and freedom to choose. At the top of the ladder of beings is God, a being who is completely in act and has no passivity. The importance of this idea for our study of Calderón is that every element that a reader or spectator of a Calderonian *comedia* experiences must have a sensorial content, for these are representations. What they ostensibly represent, however, is an order of being which points toward immateriality at its summit. Herein resides a great deal of the tension of Calderón's style, especially with respect to the *culteranista* metaphors which abound in every long speech of these plays.

In the poems of Góngora, in particular the *Soledades,* we find a tendency that can truly be called sensorial. As John Beverley says, "The details of form and function of . . . objects—the simple curve of the wooden cup, the freshness and thickness of the milk, the different sizes and weaves of the nets—are observed with an obvious attention to detail. This is hardly a language which 'alludes' to reality only to escape it in decorative embellishment and sublimation. . . ."[2] What we find in Calderón's *comedias,* on the other hand, is not precisely Gongorine, but *culteranista*: a series of stock metaphors, repeated from play to play.

Our task will now be to describe the cognitive part of the soul and the appetitive part and to contrast the two. From the former we will deduce the all-important concepts of reason and intellect, which for St. Thomas are man's highest faculties. From the appetitive soul, we will derive the notions of passions and will.

The external senses are the most passive of the cognitive faculties because they are put into action by an outside factor, by a form involving color, sound, smell, and so forth. This passivity is reflected in the Calderonian texts by the use of a pause in a character's speech, followed by a question like "¿Qué es lo que veo?" or "¿Qué escucho?" The interrogative is used to contrast the passivity of the sense perception with the mental activity of reason. Very often a dagger, a handkerchief, an offstage voice, or a battle noise suddenly breaks into the character's train of thought. These interruptions are not something the character does; they happen to him without his willing them. He undergoes a "passion" in its etymological sense of "being acted upon." Although every one of these moments in Calderón involves an active emotional response, we are concerned primarily at this stage with the fact that the character's sense organs are activated by a sensorial object which the audience perceives in most cases.

Of the five external senses, two involve direct contact of the object perceived with the sense organ: touch and taste. Aristotle notes that all animals have the sense of touch even if they possess no other.[3] For this reason, touch and taste are called the lower senses, for they require contact with the flesh, which is composed mostly of earth, the heaviest of the natural elements. Touch is the sense that receives the least attention in the *comedias* of Calderón. There is relatively little physical contact between characters onstage and there are almost no verbal descriptions of events involving touch unaccompanied by sight and hearing. Taste plays an equally minor role in Calderonian psychology.

The higher senses of smell, hearing, and sight are called so because the sense objects (odors, sounds, and colors) reach the organ through the medium of air. Of these three senses, smell and hearing are the most material since they involve some modification in the object: some physical change must occur in an object such as a flower to produce an odor[4] and there must be friction or collision of two surfaces to produce sound. Hearing is extremely important since it conveys the audible signs which we call words. Otherwise, it captures music and noises which are generally produced offstage in

Calderón's dramas, thus heightening the effect of immateriality. Disembodied voices, invisible musical instruments, gunshots, and battles reach the characters' ears without our seeing the bodily movements of people and objects which are necessary to produce them. Sight, on the other hand, involves no bodily change at all, either in the object or in the sense organ.[5] All that is required is the interposition of light and of a transparent medium. It must be remembered that light is produced by fire, the lightest and least material of the elements.

Above the five external senses in the hierarchy we find a set of internal senses, called internal because they do not directly use a bodily organ in their operation and called senses because their object is still sensorial and is not a concept. For Calderonian drama the most important of these are imagination, memory, and the *facultas aestimativa*. The first stores up sense impressions and reproduces them when the original objects which stimulated them are not present. This major difference from the external senses implies a new step in the development of dramatic characters. The audience usually shares, at least in a symbolic manner, the sensory impressions that the character is receiving at the moment of the dramatic action. If he sees a dagger lying on the floor or hears a cannon, we participate in that perception. Since imagination, on the other hand, is an internal sense, the audience can only participate in its operations through the character's words, which attempt to describe the internal impressions. A good example would be a scene in Act I of *El médico de su honra.* Don Gutierre finds an unfamiliar dagger in his house and as he embraces his wife, she sees it and recoils in horror. When he asks what is the matter, she answers: "Al verte así, presumía / que ya en mi sangre bañada, / hoy moría desangrada." A few verses later, Don Gutierre exclaims: " ¡Jesús, qué imaginación!"[6] The perception of the knife is shared by the audience, but the vision of blood must come to us through Mencía's language. Of course, this vision is inseparable from a strong emotional tone of fear which caused the hallucination. Imagination is also at work when certain characters bring to mind sensory impressions to be used as examples in discursive thinking. Segismundo brings to mind several members of the animal kingdom in his first soliloquy in order to illustrate his notion of freedom. Each example has its sensorial characteristics, which are described with *culteranista* metaphoric techniques. To the extent that Calderón loads his characters' speeches with this language, he presents them in a very un-Thomistic light as characters whose imagination carries them away temporarily from their reasoning process.

What we may call the *culteranista* factor in Calderón's language is closely intertwined with conceptual play and thus it is not allowed the free sensorial play of associations that makes for the aesthetic brilliance of Góngora's poems. The latter poet makes metaphoric connections often on the basis of physical resemblance alone, with a subsequent weakening of rational distinctions.

Calderón's language makes room for some material metaphors among its analogies and symbolisms, but in those moments when the former get out of hand, the reasoning process arrives at sophistic conclusions.

To return to a previous example, in his plea to the King of Fez, the steadfast prince Fernando provides five examples of "kings" in the natural kingdom who show mercy to human beings: among animals, the lion, the dolphin, and the eagle; among plants, the pomegranate; and among stones, the diamond. In his application of the term *rey* to the noblest of animals, Calderón is not being poetical by Renaissance standards, but rather scientific. The *Diccionario de Autoridades* gives the following supplementary definition of *rey* and does not mark it as metaphoric or allusive as in so many other cases: "Llaman asimismo al más generoso en las especies de los animales terrestres, aquatiles, volatiles u insectos: como el León, Delphín, Aguila, y Basilisco."[7] What is metaphoric about the passage is the physical equivalence made between *corona* and *guedejas*. Even the notion of a lion's clemency could be considered a fact and not a figure of speech for Calderón's age; Pliny, the great classical authority on nature, leaves that possibility open: "Leoni tantum ex feris clementia in supplices; prostratis parcit. . . ."[8] This first example of the lion, though not an apodictic proof, at least lends credibility to Fernando's thesis that *piedad* is an inherent virtue of kingship.

As he moves down the ladder of animals, however, the application of this quality becomes more and more metaphoric, although it is undeniable that the eagle can be called "king of birds" and the dolphin "king of fish" in the science of the seventeenth century. Then the analogy loses in factual validity as Fernando proceeds to call the pomegranate "queen of the fruits" and thus to consider it *piadosa*: ". . . la granada, / a quien coronan las puntas / de una corteza, en señal / de que es reina de las frutas, / envenenada marchita / los rubíes que la ilustran, / y los convierte en topacios, / color desmayada y mustia" (p. 680). Up to this point *rey* can be considered what St. Thomas would call a *nomen analogum,* in which different concepts are expressed by the same word, but in which there is a certain relationship or proportion between the concepts.[9] In Fernando's first example, a lion is to the beasts what a king is to a nation. Similar statements can be made for the next several examples. With the example of the pomegranate, however, that analogy fails and Fernando uses a material metaphor to take its place. The calyx of the fruit is likened to a crown because of the physical pattern of a circular row of spines which the two objects have in common. Then by a generalizing synecdoche (from part to whole) the concept "crown" is extended to that of "queen." This rhetorical procedure, which also constitutes a personification of the pomegranate, authorizes the predicate *piadosa,* a quality inherent in royalty, according to the thesis of Fernando's whole speech. A moral characteristic is being attributed to an object without sensation or thought. An analogy, sophistic in nature, is being made between the beneficent effects of the merciful man's acts and the effects of the pomegranate's change of color when it is tainted with poison and thereby warns the prospective eater. The device belongs to the realm of *conceptismo*. On the other hand, the *culteranista* element appears not only at the beginning of the allegorical process (*espinas de granada = corona*) but also at the end to reinforce the conceptual metaphor. The physical color change is brought to bear on the moral quality of *piedad* by the suggestion that the transition from a healthy red to a topaze yellow, a "color desmayada y mustia," is a result of the fruit's pity for the endangered eater. To raise the material intensity of the metaphor even higher, the red color becomes a part of the supposed "crown" (*rubíes*), which in turn become *topacios.*

To sum up, on the logical plane, the inductive nature of the examples taken as a whole, in which five "kings" are mentioned as proof that all kings are or should be *piadosos,* does not constitute a sound argument.[10] In the pomegranate example, the logic is further weakened by the figurative use of the term *reina.* Of course, this is only one among thousands of passages where the stretching of analogic terms to the point where they become *impropria* (in St. Thomas' terminology) makes them into enemies of the "reason" which the characters are meant to follow.[11] The function of *culteranista* language at such points is, first, to reinforce the "improper" transfers of meaning with similarities on a material plane, that is, on a level immediately evident to everyone, and, by multiplying such parallels to previously unreached heights, to convince the imagination, if not the intellect. Its second function is to express the force of will behind the character's speech and to arouse the same in the listener or reader by appealing to immediately desirable or repugnant objects, instead of to the conceptual appetite, which is harder to arouse. The idea that the pomegranate has a jewel-studded crown in Fernando's speech can only strengthen his plea, even if the logic behind it is faulty.

The syllogism behind this example could be formulated in the following way: (1) The pomegranate is merciful. (2) The pomegranate is queen (while belonging to the inferior realm of the plants). (3) Human kings and queens are or should be merciful. The first premise is, as we have seen, based on several figurative devices. The pomegranate is personified by the application of the adjective *piadosa,* which must always contain a reference to a sentient being, however indirectly. Even when we use the term to refer to an act or result, such as in the phrase *mentira piadosa,* we still imply a sentiment of mercy behind the act. Otherwise we could resort to the more general adjective *benéfico,* which can refer to happenings that are unintentionally helpful to men in distress. Thus, to make Fernando's use of the pomegranate meaningful, we must attribute feeling to the inanimate object. Góngora uses exactly the same procedure when he speaks to a wall with a chink that allows him to view his beloved and calls it "piadosa pared."[12] Yet poets of the seventeenth century, working in both the *culteranista* and *conceptista* modes, were rarely content to rest on such simple figures, and Calderón is no exception.

He seeks to "prove" that the pomegranate feels the danger of the prospective consumer of the poison by laying hold of the empirically observable color change which the fruit undergoes and by overlaying this sensorial metaphor onto the personification. Just as in the crown metaphor, we start with a synecdoche from whole to part, from the pomegranate to its color change (red to yellow). Then the same color change is pointed out in human beings and is taken as a sign of illness or violent emotion. In the case of the pomegranate both are applicable: its yellow color can be taken either as a sign that, like a human body, it is being weakened by poison, in which case the term *granada envenenada* takes on new connotations, or as a sign of its sympathy (in the etymological sense) for the eater's imminent death. These notions are reinforced by the verb *marchita,* which, after all, is *not* figurative in the case of a plant.

Yet the overall purpose of the example is to present a positive image of kingship and not to end with a sick, powerless figure. Thus Calderón adds one more layer to his allegory: the passive process of the color change is made active through the use of active verbs, *marchita* and *convierte.* It is no longer the poison which works a change in the fruit, but the fruit which transforms itself. It even shows a generous spirit of self-effacement, since it is willing to forego the more prestigious red ("rubíes que la ilustran") for the less attractive yellow, all for the sake of a human being in danger. Furthermore, the verb *convierte* in connection with two species of precious stones suggests the work of an alchemist, a powerful sage who knows and can exploit the natural properties of things. However, it must be kept in mind that while all of these notions are figurative from a twentieth-century point of view, it is difficult to determine how literally they might apply in Calderón's age, given the animistic tendencies of Renaissance books of natural science. While many of the notions found in this complex allegory can be found in Pliny, would Calderón's contemporaries also accept the Roman author's maxim: ". . . nec quaerenda ratio in ulla parte naturae, sed voluntas," which may be loosely translated, "In any part of Nature, we are not to look for a rational principle, but rather a will"?[13]

To determine how far Calderón would have considered Fernando's description of the pomegranate's properties as "false" or "figurative" would require further study of the dividing line between natural fact and fable in the minds of seventeenth-century Spaniards. The double attitude of Calderón can be seen in the words which Fernando uses to introduce the examples of the pomegranate and the diamond: "Aun entre plantas y piedras / se dilata y se dibuja / este imperio. . . ." To say "se dilata este imperio" implies that the notions used in the previous examples apply in the lower realms also; there is also *piedad* to be found there. But the verb *se dibuja* implies that the pomegranate and diamond are only symbols or figures that illustrate in pictorial form certain moral truths about the human realm.

The point of the preceding observations is that Calderón's similarity to Góngora goes beyond the mere use of "improper" turns of speech; analogies, both sound and unsound, had filled rhetorical discourses since classical times. The peculiarity of Calderón's *culteranista-conceptista* moments is the tendency to add numerous supplementary links to a traditional metaphor in order to give it further credibility and persuasive power, while never losing sight of the dissimilarities of the terms of the comparison. The resulting tension makes the allegory unforgettable and allows it to take the place of correctly formulated syllogisms.

The above metaphoric techniques depend heavily on the sensorial imagination. Memory likewise reproduces sensorial species when their original objects are not present, but unlike the imagination, it represents previously perceived objects *sub ratione praeteriti,* that is, views past objects as past.[14] It is natural that this faculty should play a large part in Calderonian drama, given the fact that, as most critics of the Baroque age have pointed out, a preoccupation with time runs through its thought and literature. The situation of Doña Mencía in the first act of *El médico* provides a good example of the effects of memory on present action. The prince Don Enrique is brought into her house after a riding accident. When Doña Mencía sees the man whom she once loved, memories come to the surface of her consciousness. Her distress throughout the scene stems from the comparison of her situation when she first met Enrique with her present condition as a married woman. She states the matter bluntly in one verse, making the contrast sharp by a pair of opposing verb tenses: "[t]uve amor, y tengo honor" (II, 36).

Strictly speaking, these words constitute an example of the *memoria aestimativa.* The second term here refers to a faculty which is akin to our modern notion of instinct.[15] It is a subrational power which perceives sense objects as immediately helpful or harmful. We will have occasion to note many instances of what Scholasticism termed *apprehensiones* in Calderón, who delights in having characters first experience a negative instinctive presentiment which is then confirmed later in the play by reason or destiny. Since every Calderonian protagonist has vital interests at stake, it follows that almost no instances of imagination or memory occur without some intervention of the *aestimativa.*

Man's highest cognitive faculty is the intellect, whose proper object is not a sensorial *simulacrum,* but a *quidditas* or essence of a material thing abstracted from its corporeal matter. A concept exists in the mind formally, although sense perception must precede intellection. The soul does not know things by knowing itself, for it comes into the world as a *tabula rasa* on which sense impressions and *quidditates* are inscribed.

Thomistic doctrine places the intellect highest among man's cognitive faculties, since its object is the most immaterial. It is therefore the most active of these in the sense that it is set in motion not simply by outside phenomena or by stored-up sense images, but by two factors: in an ultimate sense it is God who enables human beings to exercise the intellect by supplying, in the words of St. Thomas, the *lux naturalis*; in a human sense, it is the subject's own will which sets the intellect in motion. The operation of the intellect does not produce a material change in the soul, as a savory object would make a change in the tongue, so that the whole process takes place on an intentional or formal level. In this formal sense, "the soul is all existing things."[16]

This is how actuality is connected with immateriality in Aristotelianism. The forms of roundness and redness do not exist in an object which is naturally blue and square, but the intellectual soul can receive all of these forms intentionally. It has therefore a less determined and limited existence than that of other natural beings, and consequently is more *in actu* than other animals as well as plants and minerals.

The comprehension of the intelligible form is the kernel of the intellect's activity. In creatures whose intellect does not work through bodily organs, such as angels, the grasping of the essence of the intellectual object is immediate. In man, however, full comprehension is a gradual process which includes a series of acts of understanding and which is called *discursus* or reasoning. After the apprehension of the *quidditas* or general nature of the object, "the intellect must continue to discover, by degrees, the various properties and accidents of the thing together with the further elements comprised in its essence."[17] It does this through three operations: *componendo, dividendo,* and *ratiocinando.*[18] The first two involve acts of judgement, an operation whereby sense data and concepts are compared and contrasted, and affirmations and negations are made about them; the last involves the progression from one judgement to another by syllogisms.

From the foregoing description, it follows that in the cognitive realm Thomism and, as I shall argue throughout this study, the philosophical thought underlying Calderonian drama, consider knowledge of immaterial realities to be implicitly higher and more valuable than that of sensorial realities. Yet all elements in a stage performance or in a text destined for that purpose must be represented sensorially, thus creating the aforementioned tension in Calderón's style.

We can now trace the same hierarchical pattern in the appetitive faculties. As we have already noted, appetite aims at the attainment of an object in its entitative existence. The subject who experiences an appetite, rather than transforming, let us say, an apple into a mental image of redness and roundness in his mind, seeks to actually appropriate that apple in order to eat. Cognition may take place with no motion of the subject toward its object, but appetite generally leads to some form of movement. The desired (or hated) object becomes a mover, while the desiring (or hating) subject is moved.

The idea of appetition lies at the base of Aristotle's and St. Thomas' explanations of the natural world. To understand the classical meaning of appetition and to escape from modern prejudices about the word, it is necessary to keep in mind that, in natural creatures, the substantial form that gives the creature its existence also bestows upon it a natural appetite.[19] The elemental form of fire, for instance, naturally tends upward. Likewise, man's substantial form, the soul, has natural inclinations. The doctrine of appetite shows how change is related to essence in Thomism. A thing moves or is moved because of the inclination instilled in its substantial form. What it does or what it undergoes is determined by what it essentially is. Calderón struggles with the contradiction between this medieval view and the Renaissance one expressed by Cassirer in reference to Pico della Mirandola's oration on the dignity of man:

> The dignity of man cannot reside in his being, i.e., in the place allotted man once and for all in the cosmic order. The hierarchical system subdivides the world into different levels and places each being in one of these levels as its rightful place in the universe. But such a view does not grasp the meaning and the problem of human freedom. For this meaning lies in the *reversal* of the relationship we are accustomed to accepting between *being* and *acting*. The old Scholastic proposition *operari sequitur esse* is valid in the world of things. But it is the nature and the peculiarity of the human world that in it, the opposite is true. It is not being that prescribes once and for all the lasting direction which the mode of action will take. . . .[20]

The form of a thing in action becomes a "formal cause" through its natural appetite. In the age of Calderón, formal causation was still strong in theology and literature. This is one reason why analogies with natural phenomena are common in his *comedias*. Following the Petrarchan love tradition, they are full of comparisons of women's beauty to a magnet which irresistibly draws the iron or to a sun toward which the sunflower naturally turns its face. In some of these metaphors, Scholastic terminology is brought to bear. These instances of natural appetites, which were considered valid statements of cause, are extended to human affairs and are related to the frequently quoted phrase: *soy quien soy*.[21]

In animals, endowed with senses, the blind force of natural appetite becomes sophisticated. In an animal (or in a human being), which naturally desires food, the sight of an edible object excites the appetite. The object of desire is not immediately the edible object, but its sensorial representation in the sense organ. This is a higher form of appetite, since its object is not only more immaterial but is also a form within the soul of the animal, although the animal cannot avoid desiring that object. It also implies, of course, that in man the sense memory allows him to desire sense objects when they are not physically present. So even at the primitive stages of animal life, the appetitive faculties are linked to cognition. Man's natural appetites are more exactly sense appetites, for all of man's desires and aversions spring from sense knowledge. The converse is also true: that virtually no sensation occurs in a human being without activating some appetite. The poetic character of the *comedias* we will consider reflects this affective aspect of human perception. When characters describe their immediate sensations or, more often, their memories, they clothe them in a form of language which reveals, if nothing more, the basic emotional attitudes of love and hate.

Man's sense appetite can be divided into two aspects. The first has as its object an immediate sensorial good and is called the *concupiscibilis*. In all of the emotions contained in this faculty, the appetite is merely attracted or repelled by the good or evil aspects of the object. The most basic passion of this series is love (*amor*), which consists of a sense of attractiveness or affinity with a good object; its opposite is hate (*odium*), a simple sense of unattractiveness. The attraction of love provokes a movement in the lover toward the object. This is a formal movement called desire (*desiderium*) whose opposite is aversion (*fuga*). Finally, the attainment of the desired object brings the subject to rest, causing joy (*gaudium*). In the opposite case, when a hated evil actually is present, sadness (*tristitia*) arises in the subject.[22]

The fact that we are dealing with dramatic conflicts in Calderón means that our attention will be focused more sharply on the second part of man's sense appetite, the *irascibilis*, since the emotions of this faculty deal with a sensorial good or evil inasmuch as it is difficult of attainment or avoidance, inasmuch as it is *arduum*. It always looks toward an object not yet attained or an evil not yet incurred, that is, it has a more immaterial object. For this reason, and because it implies more activity than the relatively passive affections of love and hate, the *irascibilis* is a higher faculty and is closer to intellect, which is man's characteristic faculty. It comprises five basic emotions; two of them are concerned with a future good: hope (*spes*), which is a movement toward this good, and despair (*desperatio*), which is a movement away from the same, not because it is a good, since the appetite never really shuns the good, but because it is seen as too difficult of attainment. Another pair of passions deals with a future evil: fear (*timor*), which is a movement away from an imminent evil, and courage (*audacia*), which in spite of the dangers, seeks to keep that evil from occurring. In a pattern exactly converse to that of despair, courage goes toward the imminent evil, not because it is evil, which would be contradictory, but because it envisions the possibility of overcoming it. Finally, there is one emotion which has no opposite: anger (*ira*), which is a reaction against an evil actually present. [23]

A close reading of many Calderonian passages reveals a tendency on the part of many characters to classify their feelings under these and other well-defined categories. A character believes himself to have understood his emotion when he can apply the right species name to it, e.g., Herodes in Act II of *El mayor monstruo los celos,* who applies several species to his emotion without wanting to give it its real name, jealousy:

> Sea baruaridad, sea
> locura, sea ynconstançia,
> sea desesperaçión,
> sea frenesí, sea rabia,
> sea yra, sea letargo,
> o quanto después mis ansias
> quisieren; que todo quiero
> que sea, pues todo es nada,
> como no sean mis celos. . . .[24]

We are still dealing with the Scholastic tendency to consider knowledge as the correct application of predicates to subjects, but we are seeing the process in its decadent stage, since the characters are experiencing emotions that do not fit into the traditional Aristotelian categories.

The highest of man's appetitive faculties has the highest object and is called *appetitus intellectivus* or, more commonly, the will. Just as the intellect abstracts a universal concept from the multiplicity of sense data, so the will generalizes the good which is found in various sense objects and postulates a good-in-general which becomes its proper object of desire and which is called in Scholastic terminology *beatitudo.* The latter constitutes the only limit on the will: it cannot choose not to will beatitude. Of course, the gamut of situations in Calderonian *comedias* shows abundantly that the will may choose an object which ends up leading to utter unhappiness, but this is due to a failure or a limitation of the intellect. The will does not will evil *qua* evil. In Calderón this abstract scheme breaks down under the pressure of what the characters *must* do, whether it is "reasonable" or not.

The presence of a rational appetite in human beings implies that no impulse of the natural or sense appetites (except those that are physiologically involuntary) can be translated into action without the consent of the will, which guards the gates of impulse with the weapon of reason.[25] When the will is at its post, it filters each particular desire through a series of deliberations to see how far it corresponds to the definition of good-in-general or beatitude for that human being in that particular situation.[26]

The structure of human acts thus reveals itself as a series of means and ends, with the final goal of beatitude. Throughout his life, man must make decisions about alternatives presented to him. Thus the intellect intervenes in the process of deliberation, of deciding what means are best for the accomplishment of the end. The will takes part in human acts by moving the other faculties of the soul and body to carry out the means chosen by the intellect, for if the will consents to a certain end or goal, it must also necessarily will the means to that end. From these dual aspects of volition and intellection in human acts, the will receives its technical name of *appetitus intellectivus.*

In connection with this doctrine, it is important to refer to the influence of Stoicism both on medieval Scholasticism by the indirect route of the Church Fathers and on sixteenth- and seventeenth-century thought through the renewed interest in Stoic texts. In the case of Spain the most important student and propagator of these works was Quevedo, especially since he had a greater than average command of Greek. Although the original Stoic school had a system of natural science, logic, and ethics, it was not this part of their intellectual production which influenced the European Renaissance, for two reasons: in the first place, the oral teachings of the Stoa on scientific matters were largely unknown. They survived mainly through fragments or in references found in works of other ancient authors, some of which were unearthed in post-Renaissance times. Secondly, authors of the Roman world who left whole treatises or discourses (Marcus Aurelius, Seneca, Epictetus) did not regard Stoicism as a system for organizing knowledge. "They have a minimal interest in anything but ethics and see in Stoic philosophy an established system of beliefs that could guide, comfort, and support a man in the difficulties and dangers of life. They are preachers of a religion, not humble inquirers after truth."[27] It was this aspect of the school which interested Quevedo and the political writers, and which is relevant to Calderonian drama. To be more precise, we could say that it was not even Stoic ethical theory which attracted Counter-Reformation Europe, although the Stoics did have such a theory, which both resembled and differed from Aristotelian ethics. What was transmitted from Seneca and Epictetus was really an ethical procedure, a way of dealing mentally with circumstances.

Quevedo, for example, reduces the Stoic teaching to one precept, which he takes from the first chapter of Epictetus' *Encheiridion.* Whether this simplification is the result of careful sifting of various authors or is due to the paucity of texts available to Quevedo is a question for the experts in that field. The central tenet is this: all things in the world are to be divided into two categories, those which are our own (*to idion*) and are under our control, and those which are not ours (*to allotrion*) and are not under our control. The radical severity of the doctrine appears in the small list of factors which Epictetus believes we can control: our opinions of things, our choices, and our desires and aversions. Everything else is alien to our inner self: our body, our property, our reputation, and our office. Thus the attainment of wisdom consists in transforming one's mental attitudes and directing one's desires and aversions in such a way as to avoid pain and turbulence of mind. In the presence of any misfortune, the Stoic tries either to convince himself that it is not really a misfortune or to turn his mind toward the positive moral consequences which will result from it. In the presence of good fortune, the Stoic does not let himself be carried away by a sensation of pleasure which will cause pain as it fades. He renounces pleasure in order to maintain his firm moral prupose. He never blames fate or the gods for what befalls him. Thus Segismundo's first words in *La vida es sueño* ("Apurar, cielos, pretendo, / ya que me tratáis, así, / ¿qué delito cometí . . . ?") are markedly anti-Stoic.

Stoic ethical behavior concords with Thomism mainly in its negative aspect, that is, the controlling of passion through reason, which pierces apparent goods and evils to arrive at a supreme, unchangeable good. What in Stoicism is the exercise of philosophic wisdom becomes asceticism in medieval Christianity, at least as regards the pursuit of tranquillity of mind. Yet the Roman Stoics remained at this negative pole and never developed a systematic positive morality concerning man's duties in regard to the outward, "alien" goods. This is not to say that writers like Epictetus and Marcus Aurelius did not preach moral precepts that showed great similarity to Gospel teachings. They often recommended charity, humility, patience, and other such virtues. Yet correct behavior in the world was not the goal of their moral effort and it is conceivable that a Stoic could maintain his peace of mind without regard for the welfare of others. His "reason" could tell him that what seems to be a misfortune in his neighbor is only an apparent evil and that the neighbor is laboring under a delusion. Also, the Stoic might believe in an afterlife, but scorned the idea of letting a possible future reward or punishment affect his conduct. Such rewards, even if they existed, could not really belong to him, since they are external. In short, we may say that Stoic morality is generally noninstitutional; it is not a tool for building a civic community or furthering worldly interests. Although many of its greatest practitioners, such as Seneca, were men of state and were steeped all their lives in temporal affairs, nevertheless, alongside this involvement they cherished the Stoic ideal of indifference to all things except one's inner state. On the other hand, this current of thought spawned Cynics like Diogenes, who lived in squalor and shunned human community.

Readers of Calderón will immediately recognize in Stoic ideas about transitory pleasures a forefunner of the famous *desengaño* theme of Counter-Reformation Spanish literature. In this aspect Stoicism and Catholicism agree; they both strive to turn activity away from pursuing sensorially attractive goals. This, of course, is the aspect which Quevedo found readily adaptable to his Christian purposes. The corresponding doctrine of not fearing pain is also in harmony with Catholic principles, except in one important aspect. Sixteenth- and seventeenth-century Spanish Catholicism depended heavily on the fear of the pains of hell to bring about correct behavior. Yet the biblical saying that "the fear of God is the beginning of wisdom" would have been entirely repugnant to the ancient Stoics. Likewise, Ignatius Loyola's practice of having his disciples imagine one by one the tortures of the damned would have seemed base and vile to them. In Calderón's *autos* it is clear that virtue remains essentially self-centered, that is, utilitarian. In *El gran teatro del mundo,* the players carry out their roles well so that they will be well "paid" by the "company manager" at the end of the play. Even in the *comedias* this tendency can be seen indirectly: when Segismundo awakes from the pleasures and pains of this world, he knows he will be assigned to eternal pleasures or pains in accordance with his temporal conduct. Thus the Stoics follow a more austere reason by being willing to forego pleasure and pain entirely. They do this by correcting the subjective attitudes that make events pleasurable or painful.

It is clear from this brief sketch that in many aspects Calderón's secular characters can be considered negative examples of Stoic doctrine. In general, if characters in a drama were to follow Stoic precepts to the limit, the plot would come to a standstill. Even for the most virtuous characters, moral duty always has a positive content and is never a matter of maintaining indifference. They may, like the Stoics, be required to reject false goals and discriminate between the apparent and the real, but the supreme good they discover (or fail to discover) at the end of their trajectory always involves definite duties to be performed and definite sins to be avoided in society. It involves doing one thing and not another. This is the opposite of the Stoic procedure of reducing all possible modes of activity to inner representations.

Thus Calderonian characters use patterns of reasoning that, while bearing a resemblance to Stoic procedures, also contain important differences. The following are a few examples of thoughts used in the asides and soliloquies of the *comedias*.

1. The character consoles himself for the loss of some beloved person or object to another by reminding himself that the new possessor will eventually lose his possession also, since no possession is eternal. If the thought thereby reduces the "disproportionate" value of the object of desire in the character's eyes, it is truly Stoic; but if it is accompanied by a long-term hope of recovering the possession one day, it loses its Stoic kernel and reveals an underlying passion. It becomes a corollary to the law of the wheel of Fortune, in which the wheel comes back to its starting point and restores the fallen to their high position. This thought pattern derives part of its appeal from its similarity to the Christian idea that it is necessary to pass through humiliation in order to arrive at glory and that the meek shall inherit the earth. In the political drama *La gran Cenobia,* which will be treated more fully in Chapter 3, Decio, the Roman general, is stripped of his sword by the emperor Aureliano, after the former confesses that he was not able to defeat the beautiful queen Cenobia in battle. In a soliloquy, Decio first curses the emperor, then realizes that he is wasting his breath, since his words do not further his cause in any way. He represses his passion, not by declaring its object (Cenobia) to be intrinsically worthless, but by reasoning that Aureliano either will be defeated like him or, if victorious, will one day be toppled from his fortunate state. This will be accomplished by the constant revolution of time. Here the passion is checked in order that it may obtain a more satisfying vengeance later.

2. The frequent Calderonian act of penetrating behind appearances to reality, although it owes much to Stoicism, has an underlying base which is purely Christian. Justina in *El mágico prodigioso,* whose case will be dealt with fully in Chapter 5, resists the apparent pleasurable sensations that the Devil presents to her and expresses her resistance in almost Stoic terms: ". . . esta pasión / . . . llevó la imaginación, / pero no el consentimiento."[28] This inner consent to mental representations was one of the Stoics' most important ethical concepts. Yet her reason for resisting can be found in the words, "Es muy costoso ese gusto" (I, 202). It is not in her eternal self-interest to risk her salvation for an unreal temporal pleasure.

From all these remarks on Stoicism, it is clear that the radical methods of controlling passions espoused by the Stoics could not be applied to Calderón's dramatic world, since they would have posed a danger to the values which do *not* come under reason's scrutiny in his plays. How could one of Calderón's military characters look upon his battles as valueless by following Marcus Aurelius' dictum that "Alexander, Pompeius and Gaius Caesar times without number utterly destroyed whole cities, and cut to pieces many myriads of horse and foot on the field of battle, yet the day came when they too departed this life"?[29] How could a woman like Doña Mencía in *El médico de su honra,* while struggling to preserve her honor in the eyes of the world, say, again with Marcus Aurelius, "Look at . . . the empty echo of acclamation, and the fickleness and uncritical judgment of those who claim to speak well of us . . ." (p. 71)? Even if the characters did perform these transvaluations of values, they could not then proceed to affirm that their acts would not result in eternal salvation or damnation. Their desires and aversions could not be repressed to that extent.

By analyzing the structure of the acts of one character within a particular passage of a Calderonian tragedy, we can see a reflection of the Scholastic description of the interplay of intellect and will. In the second half of Act II of *El mayor monstruo,* Mariene, the wife of the Tetrarch, faces a situation which puts into action all her cognitive and affective faculties. Her husband, Herodes, who has been condemned to death in Alexandria by the emperor Octaviano, has sent a message back to Jerusalem to the effect that as soon as the news of his death reaches home, his trusted advisor should kill Mariene, since the Tetrarch cannot bear the thought that Octaviano might come to Jerusalem and try to marry his widow. When the messenger arrives at Mariene's garden, a fellow servant and former lover spies him and immediately believes that the death warrant is a love message to the messenger from another woman. The lovers struggle over the paper and end up tearing it into pieces. Mariene comes into the garden, orders the two servants away, and proceeds to pick up the scraps of paper. As the written message is progressively revealed to her, her emotion changes and is intensified.[30] The first three words she reads are *muerte, honor,* and *Mariene,* a combination which suggests possible horrors and which produces fear in her spirited orexis (*irascibilis*). As her knowledge becomes more complete, the fear is compounded with anger which reacts against an accomplished fact: that her husband desires her destruction. She falls for the moment into sadness at her plight: " ¡O ynfelize vna y mil veçes / la que se ve aborreçida / de la cosa que más quiere!" (p. 104). Then she turns back to discursive inquiry to try to comprehend the causes of the message she has stumbled upon. She uses the verbal form of an apostrophe to her absent husband, and her thought follows a pattern of syllogistic argument: "O te quiero o no" (p. 105). If she does not love him, would it not be nobler for him to forget a woman who no longer cares for him? If she does love him, is it not self-evident that, upon hearing of his death, she will kill herself without his having to give an order? In all its aspects, her husband's act is condemnable, so a new wave of anger rises in her. "Mas ¡ay! que en llegando a este / término, no sé qué nuevo / espíritu me enfureçe . . ." (p. 105). The use of the word *término* has a definite Scholastic and logical implication; the mind has reached a judgement, a resting place in its discourse, and now the emotions react to the conclusion. The passion of hatred dominates her soul and the will consents to pronouncing a curse on her husband. Her passions are "calling her to arms" (*me tocan al arma*), which is a metaphor for the way in which animal passions move the intellect and body. Now the deliberative stage is over and hatred is ready to take vengeance. In the middle of her curse, however, she stops short and reminds herself that "vna cosa es ser quien soy, / y otra ofenderme él" (p. 106). Reason enters again in the form of social standing and marital obligations which check the flow of anger. Mariene's mind is now evenly divided between two equally powerful affections: one is the anger caused by the wrong inflicted on her by Herodes; the other is the pity caused by long-standing marital love supported by royal duties and personal queenly dignity. The final step in the process, which actually occurs in the interval between the second and third acts, is the practical reconciliation of these mental forces in one plan of action. Her *ingenio* must find a way of pardoning as a queen and avenging herself as a wife.

The interplay of thoughts and passions, which we have just described and which acts as fuel for dramatic conflict in countless instances in Calderón's plays, also illustrates a final Scholastic issue: the relative nobility of intellect over will. While the Scotist school of medieval thought places will as man's highest faculty, St. Thomas insists that, absolutely speaking, intellect is superior to will.[31] There is a relative sense in which the will is superior, since its universal object, which is the good, is more all-encompassing than truth, which is the intellect's object. Also, it can be argued that the will puts into operation both the intellect and the other faculties of the soul and body, therefore it is more perfect.[32] Thirdly, it can be said that the will is superior inasmuch as its object is an external good in its concrete existence, not the formal species which the intellect apprehends. Yet the major Thomistic tradition, which carried over into the Spanish Counter-Reformation theologians in whose works Calderón was schooled, definitely placed human intellect higher than will, basing its argument on the principle of immateriality which we have already explored.[33] In the ranking of human powers, the rank of the proper object of a faculty determines that faculty's relative worth. The object of the will is an external good or evil, that is, something not yet appropriated or united to the desiring subject. As long as the good that man's will seeks is material, its attainment implies movement, either mental or locomotive.

The object of the intellect, on the other hand, is nonmaterial. It exists in a formal mode within the subject's soul. So in reference to natural beings of the mineral, vegetable, and animal kingdoms as well as in reference to human beings, it is implicitly more noble for a person to know them than to desire or hate them. In reference to superior beings such as angels and God, the reverse is true: for man it is more valuable to love God than to know about him.

In many studies on Calderón it has been shown how his secular theater is based on the principle just stated. These plays have been considered basically intellectualistic in the Scholastic philosophical sense of the word. It has been asserted that, in accordance with the medieval theological tradition, Calderón presents a dramatic world in which reason, in its function as controller and harmonizer of the passions, is still a sure guide to blessedness and in which the violation of this principle leads to harm or destruction both for individual characters and for social groups.[34]

In this study, my contention will not be that this view of Calderón is false, but rather that it only tells one side of a more complex story. Parker suggests this complexity with his idea of "Christian tragedy," which points in two directions: to the hierarchical universal order of the *autos* which cannot but permeate the *comedias,* and to the irrepressible human passions which bring down catastrophic consequences.[35] The difficulty with this conception is that the deviations from the Christian absolute are considered as abstract human sins or improper uses of free will rather than patterns of behavior which are necessitated by the noble status of the characters. Secondly, no attention is given to the possibility that the passions, rather than being mere deviations from a static absolute standard, are the building blocks of even the most noble endeavors. Neither in Calderón's works nor in those of most seventeenth-century Spanish authors does this idea find direct expression; we are not dealing with a dramatist who innovates in philosophy. Yet his characters behave in ways which often prefigure the idea that the will is not merely a guardian who carries out the decrees of the intellect, inspired ultimately by grace, but an energizing force which causes changes in the external world. For this idea of passions as active to be asserted in philosophy, the hierarchical cosmology and social doctrine of the Middle Ages had to be eroded, which was unthinkable in Calderón's Spain. I cannot disagree with Parker and others that, insofar as it is possible to determine the "beliefs" of an author who has left us virtually nothing but dramatic writings, Calderón's beliefs adhered to the Scholastic doctrines I have outlined. What this study proposes to show is that there is a discrepancy between ideology and the behavior of the dramatic characters. Parker never suggests that the passions which seem *desordenadas* from the Scholastic point of view might be based on other motives which in the Renaissance and Baroque ages begin to compete with moral theology: reasons of the heart and reasons of state.

2

Matrimonial Plays

Various critics have tried to show that the honor code is presented in the Calderonian dramas as a tragic phenomenon which brings ruin to the husbands who practice it and which parodies true religious and social values.[1] There are three aspects of the Thomistic order that are relevant to this problem. The first is the concept of hierarchy, according to which the beings of the universe are ordered one to another, each one having an immediate end in another being and finally in God, the highest good. Some beings are therefore more perfect than others, but each being is to fulfill its purpose by relating itself in a proper way to the creatures above and below it. It has been contended that the jealous husbands who take revenge are unaware of, or are consciously ignoring, their place in the wider fabric of existence.

The second Thomistic aspect to be applied is that of judgement. These characters have a disposition to judge wrongly the real situation around them, in other words to replace reality (*ser*) with an appearance (*parecer*) confirmed by their passions. This distortion operates not only in relation to their wives' behavior, but also in relation to their own conduct in taking revenge.[2]

Finally, the honor code in Calderón presupposes an attitude toward language which contradicts Scholasticism. There is an equation made by several "dishonored" husbands between the utterance of such words as *agravio* and *celos,* and an actually committed act of adultery. Talking about these matters comes to be an offense in itself, which in turn must be avenged. This divorce of verbal sign from reality constitutes a conceptual framework for the understanding of the values implied in the *código de honor.*

The honor plays present the most particular and individual stage of the hierarchy of beings with which the Calderonian *comedias* are concerned: the institution of matrimony. We are dealing here with the smallest human social cell in its initial stage. No birth or rearing of children is involved in the marriages of Don Gutierre or of Don Lope de Almeida. Both marriages are newly formed and involve only the love and friendship between husband and wife and the relationship of the couple to the community.

The basic purpose of honor in the institution of matrimony would seem to be that of maintaining a right relationship between a married couple and other members of society. Sexual relations in marriage are exclusive, and honor, being a *testimonia de excellentia alicujus* in its Thomistic definition,[3] bears witness in this case to the purity of marriage and to the absence of adultery. The husbands in these plays are right in believing that honor is not granted by oneself, but by others. On the wife's part, the *esplendor* of her honor testifies to the fact that she is faithful to her husband, and on the husband's part, defending his honor means that he is ready to punish anyone who tries to commit adultery with his wife. Since honor should be tributary to merit, it follows that a happy and faithful marriage should be a higher end than the preservation of honor *qua* other's tribute. So the social code which serves as an axiom to the whole action of the play does not follow the Christian pattern in its ordering of means and ends.

The same reversal of priorities occurs in the husbands' thoughts and actions when they finally decide to take revenge. The question of justifiable vengeance, so important in the honor plays, is intimately connected with that of hierarchy in Thomism. The most relevant text is the portion of the *Summa Theologiae* entitled "De vindicatione" (IIaIIae, qu. 108). The first article deals with the question of the cases in which vengeance is lawful. Contrary to modern expectations, the oft-quoted verse in Deuteronomy attributed to God ("Vengeance is mine and I will repay") does not lead St. Thomas to find all vengeance or punishment unlawful. He replies to those who insist on this biblical verse that "[o]ne who exacts vengeance of the wicked in keeping with his own station does not arrogate to himself what is God's; rather he simply exercises a God-given power."[4] One's position in the hierarchy, therefore, determines under what circumstances and against whom one may take revenge. The "husbands of honor," taking their cue from the generalized honor code under which they live, have already settled this question in their minds. They possess honor, which is referred to in various passages as "eternal honor" or as a sun whose splendor cannot be dimmed, and in the *Alcalde de Zalamea* as a "patrimony of the soul." These expressions make honor into a semidivine quality which participates somehow in eternity and which confers upon its possessors a power to judge and to execute. Nothing could be farther from the Thomistic definition of honor as a "testimony to someone's excellence" which can be destroyed. Calderón's protagonists struggle with this antinomy of honor as eternal yet fragile as glass.

The power to take vengeance into one's hands is conferred by noble blood and the honor code, which are social determinants but which are internalized by the protagonists, who thus become self-appointed judges and executioners. Far from receiving their authority from God or written law, they do not even want others to know of their revenge. It is evident to what extent these husbands usurp what was deemed to be God's prerogative in their threats of vengeance. Man, according to Christian tradition, can kill the body but only God can kill the soul. Don Lope de Almeida, however, claims that if he suspected anyone of harming his honor, "no tuviera, ¡vive Dios!, / vida que no le quitara, / sangre que no le vertiera, / almas que no le sacara; / y éstas rompiera después, / a ser visibles las almas."[5] Although this passage is best seen as figurative, it still indicates the passion of pride which wants to arrogate to itself the knowledge and power over souls that belong only to their creator.

It is also necessary to consider the intention of the avenger, since even an act which produces good results is vitiated if the motive of the agent is evil. The first article of *Quaestio 108* also deals with this subject. "Vengeance . . . can be lawful . . . if the intention of the avenger is aimed chiefly at a good to be achieved by punishing a wrongdoer" (XLI, 117). Three proper motives are listed: (1) correction of the wrongdoer, (2) restraining him for the safety of others, and (3) safeguarding the right and doing honor to God. Clearly the "husbands of honor" have none of these motives. In one sense they do seek to carry out the last two intentions. They see themselves as ridding their noble class of a blot that might infect others with the same disease, although in trying to safeguard honor, they sacrifice human lives.

St. Thomas mentions several evil motives for punishing wrongdoers, among them the following: "Should [the avenger's] intention be centered chiefly upon the evil done to the recipient and is satisfied with that, then the act is entirely unlawful" (XLI, 117). Strange to say, Don Gutierre in *El médico de su honra* and Don Lope de Almeida very seldom fall into this temptation. It is remarkable that direct expression of hatred for the men who threaten their marital peace occupies very little of their speech. Just like in a man who punishes crimes against himself because they are offensive to God's law rather than because he has been personally wronged, so there is a tragic nobility in these husbands who, at the moment of carrying out their vengeance, do so in the name of honor. Their stated intention is toward an ideal rather than toward personal satisfaction. They are acting in the same way as Lope de Vega's Duke of Ferrara who tries to make himself and the audience believe that his personal *venganza* is really a judicial *castigo*.

The last article of *Quaestio 108* deals with the issue "whether vengeance is to be taken on those whose offense is involuntary" (XLI, 125). St. Thomas argues that since punishment, considered as a *poenale malum,* should be administered only to those who commit sin and Augustine says that every sin is voluntary, punishment should only be inflicted on those whose offense is voluntary. The two wives in the honor plays we are studying, Doña Mencía and Doña Leonor, can be accused of imprudence, for their repeated appeals to their suitors not to persecute them any longer only make them look more guilty, but their will does not entertain the intention of committing adultery nor do they ever commit such an act. So the definition of punishment, according to this Thomistic text, as a "restoration of the balance of justice" (XLI, 127), is not fulfilled. If punishment is considered as a social medicine which inflicts some pain in order to bring about a greater cure, St. Thomas concedes that sometimes a person is punished without having sinned, but he warns that in every case "we must be sure that no remedy ever destroy a greater good in order to bring about a lesser good, even as medicine never blinds an eye in order to heal a blister" (XLI, 129). This last metaphor used by St. Thomas describes exactly what the "husbands of honor" have done. According to the medieval hierarchy of being, spiritual goods are intrinsically higher than temporal or corporeal goods. There is a vestige of this notion in Don Gutierre's mind when he warns his wife in a letter that, although it is too late to save her life, she has two hours in which to confess her sins and prepare for a Christian death. Both husbands, nevertheless, are willing to sacrifice their wives for what they consider to be a spiritual good, honor. The sad examples of the secondary characters of these plays, Doña Leonor in *El médico* and Don Juan de Silva in *A secreto agravio,* show us how temporal honor can be, notwithstanding the noblemen's expressions about *eterno honor.* So both protagonists have administered poison instead of medicine. They have exalted a lesser good above a greater.

In discussing the motives, the rationalizations, the emotional attitudes, and the methods of the avengers of honor, Dunn and Wardropper have observed a common thread which can be generalized in the following way: (1) In each case something real and valid in its own sphere is vitiated by transference to another sphere of being. Such is the case with honor, which has its importance in social relations and political life, but which becomes monstrous when made into a "spiritual" attribute or a god. (2) Likewise, a good of any kind becomes an evil when it is sought after with no regard for any other good.

The husbands of honor, like many other Calderonian protagonists, are faced with situations which require them to make a judgement about certain facts which their senses present to them. These facts are usually fragmentary. We will see, however, that the predisposition to suspicion which is inherent in Calderonian honor inclines the judgement in one direction before all the evidence is fully considered. The phenomenon is similar to that of a biased judge in a courtroom except that all the deliberation takes place internally.[6] By the evidence that the husband possesses through direct experience or through hearsay, he must judge whether his wife has been unfaithful or not. This step is crucial, for if the judgement on this point is affirmative, the honor code dictates certain drastic action to be taken immediately. We should examine, therefore, in Scholastic terms, the mechanism by which judgements are made on such practical matters and then see whether Calderón's protagonists follow this procedure.

Thomism teaches that the principal instrument of the mind in reasoning is the syllogism, the combining of propositions to form new conclusions. It claims that if the love of truth guides the train of reasoning and care is taken in the statement of premises and conclusions, then true knowledge can be attained. Love of controversy, egotism, and other passions cloud the search for truth.[7] This can be said to be the case of Don Lope de Almeida and Don Gutierre. Their primary motivation is not love of truth but rather fear of dishonor, which produces monologues that preserve a basic syllogistic structure, but which break off reasoning when emotion overwhelms them. They cannot escape from their preoccupations even at the beginning of their discourse; they cannot get an objective viewpoint on their own predicament or *hacer de sí otra mitad*, as Don Lope would like to be able to do.

Thus when Don Gutierre in the second act calms his initial emotion and sets out to examine his situation rationally, he does so hoping to find extenuating circumstances for the incriminating evidence. He even prays to God to help him find a *descargo*: "Pero vengamos al caso, / quizá hallaremos respuesta. / ¡Oh, ruego a Dios que la haya! / ¡Oh, plegue a Dios que la tenga!" (II, 73). His reason proceeds timidly, not wanting to carry the reasoning process too far, for it might bring him to a conclusion which his honor would take as final evidence requiring vengeance. One by one he finds excuses for all the incriminating circumstances: his wife was the one who informed him of a man's presence in the house; the light might have been blown out by an accidental wind and not by Mencía; the dagger he has found may belong to a servant, even though its hilt pattern matches that of Enrique's sword. At this point Gutierre utters an aside ("¡Ay dolor mío!") which seems to have been placed there by Calderón to show the audience that the character's will wants to believe in its own reasonings but that it cannot convince itself because of the fear that paralyzes its mental movements.[8] Reason continues to explain away the events of the previous night until it hits on a good cover-all explanation: perhaps a bribed servant has let Enrique into the house. At this juncture Don Gutierre makes a strange exclamation: "¡Oh, cuánto me estimo haber / hallado esta sutileza!" (II, 74). It is not the clear sense of reason which evaluates the probability of the explanation, but rather the passion which immediately seizes upon the same as a means of satisfying itself. The consideration of this possibility soothes the fear rather than aggravating it, so naturally Don Gutierre judges it to be conclusive, although he calls it a logical *sutileza*, a thin or insubstantial argument. His reasoning becomes a mockery of Scholastic disputation since it uses arguments to prove a conclusion which has already been accepted by faith. He believes that he has satisfactorily completed his discourse: "Y así acortemos discursos . . ." (II, 74).

At this point Gutierre's desire for marital peace wins out over his fear, although he makes this decision through passion and not through wise judgement. He resolves that Mencía's honor cannot be stained, but several verses later the fear returns: "Pero sí puede, mal digo. . . ." Not having real proof for or against infidelity, this suspicious fear refuses to be permanently calmed. Yet Don Gutierre's reason still has enough strength to make him realize that the best method in such doubtful cases is to suspend judgement until further evidence is gathered.[9] Furthermore, as a husband he has an obligation to keep his marriage intact, just as a doctor has the responsibility to preserve the health of the body. He acts here as a physician intent on preventing disease in his marriage, although we can see in this monologue the beginnings of the cruelty of the "surgeon of his honor." In short, the rhetorical devices of questions, syllogisms, asides, and pauses lend tension to the soliloquy, the tension of reason struggling to maintain a train of thought against ill-contained emotions that break through to the surface at various intervals.

The presence of the passions is revealed principally by what has been called the poetic character of Calderón's dramas.[10] In the monologue we have just been analyzing, it is noteworthy that Don Gutierre uses syllogistic thought until the moment when fear of dishonor returns to his mind. At that point his language suddenly becomes metaphoric. Honor is compared to the sun, whose light can be dimmed, if not extinguished, by a passing cloud. In Scholastic terms this constitutes an analogy, an inductive transference of a relation between terms of one set to those of another. The sun analogy in this case is poetically effective, for it expresses perfectly Don Gutierre's fear of dishonor. But the Thomistic dialectician would ask himself whether the analogy holds logically, for it is clear that "true" honor is not tarnished by gossip or incriminating appearances, just as the sun's light is not really eclipsed by a cloud but only seems so. Wardropper has pointed out that the entire extended metaphor of the *médico* has a poetic logic of its own and does not necessarily follow the logic of Christian ethics. So it seems that at several points in the monologues of the "husbands of honor," judgements are made on the basis of analogies in which the terms of one relation are poetically applied to another case; these also are cases where a passion prevents the reasoning process from being carried any further. In the strange combination of Scholastic reasoning and *culteranista* poetry which Calderón offers us, the distinction between analogy and metaphor is blurred. On one hand, Don Gutierre is only multiplying analogies by comparing honor to a sun or to glass. This resemblance in turn makes us aware that the reverse can also be affirmed: that reasoning about spiritual realms of being (including honor) is a kind of metaphor and in poetic metaphor there are no rules of proper and improper comparisons such as we find in medieval theology. The very fact that these husbands imitate traditional forms of reasoning means that the validity of Scholasticism does not escape unscathed from Calderón's use of it in his *comedias*.

Don Lope de Almeida's second act monologue has many structural elements in common with Don Gutierre's, but it differs in that Don Lope does not set out to find answers to his objections at first, but lets himself fall into a series of anguished questions. His mind is more strongly occupied by his dishonor, because he pronounces and reacts to the *celos* before making a rational investigation of the case. When he does start to dialogue with himself ("¿Quién es este / caballero castellano . . . ?" [I, 44]), it is clear that his mind is predisposed to accusation since he, like Don Gutierre, falls into metaphoric language. He compares the unknown "suitor" to a sunflower which drinks in the beams of his honor's sun. This metaphor makes his previous question merely rhetorical, for we realize that he already considers this stranger to be sucking away his honor. Once again the poetry is dazzling, but Don Lope is not really trying to find out the truth. He manages to gain the presence of mind to consider the other side of the argument, for the reason that "el honor no quiere / por tan sutiles discursos / condenar injustamente" (I, 45). Thus Don Lope realizes, like Don Gutierre, that his mind is dealing with very subtle and delicate problems of interpretation that allow for various solutions. While the hero of *El médico* was overjoyed to find a *sutileza* which would justify his stance, Don Lope wants to put his reasoning on a firmer footing. He seriously considers the interpretations which his wife and his friend have given to their own words. Both of them have explained in perfectly rational terms their reasons for advising him to stay or leave. He finds explanations for the presence of the Castilian stranger near his house, and finally comes to the same conclusion as Don Gutierre: "Leonor es quien es y yo / soy quien soy . . ." (I, 46). The similar pattern continues in the exclamatory reaction ("Pero sí puede, ¡ay de mí!") and in the introduction of the sun metaphor. Don Lope manages to suspend judgement until he can "tocar la ocasión / de mi vida y de mi muerte . . ." (I, 47). These last words are a self-fulfilling prophecy, for although this dubious suspicion would not be a matter of life and death under other social circumstances, we know that the nobleman Don Lope is going to make it so.

The moment when Don Lope lets the suspended judgement fall on the side of accusation slips by the reader without his noticing it. At the end of Act II, the protagonist's patience is stretched to the limit by his finding the Castilian stranger in his house, although the latter offers a plausible explanation for his presence. Before Don Lope orders the stranger out of his house, he has an aside in which, even at this juncture, he finds he can still suspend judgement. The stranger's excuses may be true after all, so he tells his mind: "sufre, disimula y calla." He shows the stranger out of the house, warning him at the same time not to speak of his presence there to anyone. The act ends with the characteristic Calderonian technique of having each character in rapid succession reveal his emotion of the moment in a short aside. The final word is Don Lope's and runs thus: "Desta manera, / el que de vengarse trata, / hasta mejor ocasión, / sufre, disimula y calla" (I, 66). Suddenly he is talking of vengeance; the passions have yielded to the pressure of the aristocratic ethic and have given their assent to a judgement of guilty. There really is no final convincing incident that persuades the reason. We must assume that all through the second act a growing feeling of dishonor, only half-recognized, has been present in Don Lope's mind and now makes the judgement for him without his full rational assent. The patience, prudence, and silence which he swore to keep earlier in order not to make a false judgement now will be used to act on the false judgement made unconsciously and blindly.

From all the passages just cited, a general picture can be constructed of how the "husbands of honor" handle the dilemmas of thought in the first two acts of both *El médico* and *A secreto agravio*. The end of the second act in both cases contains a suspenseful turning point. We have already quoted Don Lope's decision to keep a silent lookout for an opportunity to avenge his dishonor; Don Gutierre makes a similar comment: "Pues médico me llamo de mi honra, / yo cubriré con tierra mi deshonra" (II, 86). For both men the period of investigation and judgement is over and the time for action has come. The third act will reveal the "intellectual virtues" of the husbands, their *prudencia* and *discreción*,[11] in avenging themselves while keeping their dishonor a secret. It is the shrewdness of their plans that draws forth the awed exclamations of "¡Notable sujeto!" and "el caso más notable que la antigüedad celebra" in the final scenes. The reader or spectator, however, who is privy to all the monologues and asides of the first two acts, knows the interior process of judgement that has led to that action. He knows that the same mental acuteness used in the revenge was not exercised in the decision to avenge, and that at the root of the action is a passion which controls the man instead of his controlling it. The active power of reason only really begins to function in the third act after the passive powers of fear and hatred have swayed the mind in a certain direction and fixed its decision.

There remains to be considered a special case of judgement of evidence which adds a twist to these two plays, i.e., the correct interpretation of words. The most general and perhaps the most important idea we can state about language in relation to the Calderonian character is contained in the dictum of Aristotle in *De interpretatione*: "[T]hose that are in vocal sound are signs (*sýmbola*) of passions in the soul. . . ."[12] Even when there is conscious deception through language (which happens quite often in Calderón), the language of the characters expresses and exteriorizes their thoughts and feelings, especially in soliloquies. The passage of Aristotle continues thus: "But the passions of the soul, of which vocal sounds are the first signs, are the same for all; and the things of which passions of the soul are likenesses are also the same." The "passions of the soul" should be taken to refer to the simple conceptions of the understanding which are abstracted from sense data and in which there is no affirmation or negation; and the "things," to the objective reality outside the mind.[13] These two elements must agree, since Boethius points out that "nisi enim quandam similitudinem rei quam quis intelligit in animae ratione patiatur, nullus est intellectus."[14] It is in the reasoning process, where the combining and dividing of sense impressions and simple concepts takes place, that there can be either truth, an "adaequatio rei et intellectus," or falsehood.

The reason forms judgements (true or false) and articulates them in words which are heard by the speaker himself and by others. If the judgement is true, then its communication spreads knowledge and wisdom, but if it is false and is received verbally by others, then ignorance is propagated. The unreasonable assumption of the honor code is that any judgement concerning a wife's infidelity or a husband's acquiescence will automatically be received as true by other noblemen; therefore it is imperative to the honor of these husbands that no statement to this effect, whether true or false, be uttered. Hence the concern about what is said or left unsaid, even in soliloquies. Keeping in mind the above arguments, let us examine more passages from the second act soliloquies of Don Lope and Don Gutierre.

As we have seen, for both of the husbands those soliloquies constitute their first attempt to consider their situation at length and take stock of the state of their honor. Don Gutierre ends his speech with a set of words about speaking and the voice, which are placed much earlier in Don Lope's monologue. In both cases, the remarks are inspired by the utterance of a word which the protagonists wanted to avoid saying: *celos*. The train of thought stops short and there is a pause in the speech, indicating that the audible enunciation of the word has caused a profound emotion in the speaker. Don Gutierre then goes on to ask himself in disbelief:

> ¿Celos dije?
> ¡Qué mal hice! Vuelva, vuelva
> al pecho, la voz. Mas no,
> que si es ponzoña que engendra
> mi pecho, si no me dió
> la muerte (¡ay de mí!) al verterla,
> al volverla a mí podrá;
> que de la víbora cuentan,
> que la mata su ponzoña,
> si fuera de sí la encuentra.
> ¿Celos dije? ¿Celos dije?
> Pues basta; que cuando llega
> un marido a saber que hay
> celos, faltará la ciencia;
> y es la cura postrera
> que el médico de honor hacer intenta.
>
> (II, 75)

The peculiar function of language in this passage is embodied in the metaphor of the snake which can be killed by its own poison. Spoken language has the purpose of permitting communication of inner thoughts and feelings, as indicated in our quotation from Aristotle. Once a word or sentence is uttered, the meaning it conveys is made public. Don Gutierre repents of having uttered the word *celos* because he himself has ears and can hear his own speech, which brings home to him a concept he did not wish to make known even to himself. On the other hand, as indicated earlier in his speech, he feels the need to relieve the emotional pressure within him by means of verbal *quejas,* for at the beginning of the speech, he draws a parallel between the tears which flow from the eyes and the laments which the voice pronounces, both of which express the heart's pain.

The lack of another human being with whom to communicate one's grief is expressed more dramatically by Don Lope:

> ¿Quién hiciera de sí otra
> mitad, con quien él pudiese
> descansar? Pero mal digo:
> ¿Quién hiciera cuerdamente
> de sí mismo otra mitad,
> porque en partes diferentes,
> pudiera la voz quejarse
> sin que el pecho lo supiese?
>
> (I, 42)

This husband comes up against the same frustration: he cannot share his grief even with himself, for the voice only reminds him of something he does not want to acknowledge. He vainly wishes that he could express himself without hearing his own voice: "Fuera todo lenguas, fuese / nada oídos, nada ojos, / porque oprimido de verse / guardado, no rompa el pecho, / y como mina reviente" (I, 42).

Don Gutierre's reason needs words to express its doubts, but the passions react violently at the mention of certain words. Until the moment that *celos* is mentioned, he has acted like a prudent doctor, prescribing in this first, critical stage of the disease of dishonor the preventative medicine of silence.[15] The key word, though, upsets his rational decision, for when a husband "finds out" that there is jealousy involved, his wisdom (or medical science) gives way and he is ready to perform the *cura postrera* whose nature the reader discovers in the third act. We can measure the extent to which Don Gutierre's fear of dishonor has overwhelmed him by his last statement. He has not "found out" anything definite about his wife's conduct. The "discovery" he makes is that of a word, a *respiración fácil* as Don Lope calls it, which he takes for a reality. Moreover, the word comes from himself and not from the mouth of another. It is a token of his own "passion of the soul." Unlike the word "adultery," which at least refers, truly or falsely, to an exterior situation, *celos* refers purely to a state of mind. The *Diccionario de Autoridades* defines it thus: "[V]ale la sospecha, inquietud, y rezelo, de que la persona amada haya mudado, ò mude su cariño, ò afición, poniendola en otra."[16] This definition, however, does not correspond to what Don Gutierre means when he says, "Tengo celos." It is not only the fact that the loved one may be estranged that causes the passion, but also, and perhaps most importantly, that others will find out about it.

Besides dealing with their own speech, the husbands in the honor plays encounter difficult situations in which they must start from other characters' language and infer from it the emotions of their interlocutors.[17] Hence a need for the constant exercise on their part of the science of interpretation or, in Aristotelian language, hermeneutics. In both *El médico* and *A secreto agravio* the husbands' second act monologues are preceded by the abrupt exit of another character or characters, who leave without making their feelings clear. In the former play, Prince Enrique takes leave of Don Gutierre without saying a word, after hearing the latter warn him away from Doña Mencía in a veiled way, although there is a short aside which partially expresses Enrique's thoughts to the audience. Don Gutierre interprets the prince's silence in this fashion: "Nada Enrique respondió, / sin duda se convenció / de mi razón" (II, 72). In the latter play, Don Lope faces a thornier dilemma. When he asks his wife and his best friend whether he should join the king's military expedition, the former counsels him to go and the latter counsels him to stay. To Don Lope, the advice of each is exactly the opposite of what it should be: "¿En más razón no estuviera / que aquí mudados viniesen / de mi amigo y de mi esposa / consejos y pareceres?" (I, 45). A wife should naturally want her husband to stay at home, and a friend, naturally concerned with his friend's reputation, would encourage him to perform an action which would increase his honor and wealth. Don Lope still has enough reason to consider that there is an explanation for these incriminating circumstances, given by Doña Leonor and Don Juan in their own speeches before leaving the stage. Doña Leonor says she wants to overcome her womanly sentiments and advise her husband in a courageous, manly way: "[Q]ue no quiero que se diga / que las cobardes mujeres / quitan el valor a un hombre, / cuando es razón que le aumenten" (I, 40). She says she is speaking as another person different from herself, instead of expressing her true feelings: "[M]as como ajena lo dice, / si como propia lo siente" (I, 40). Don Juan reasons that his friend has already performed enough military service for his king and deserves to exchange the laurels of Mars for the palm of peace. Both of these arguments are valid and indicate a noble nature in wife and friend, but the predisposition of Don Lope's mind, which we apprehend through the aside he utters upon entering at the beginning of the second act ("¡Ay honor, mucho me debes!" [I, 37]), suggests another monstrous interpretation which is perfectly consistent with the few facts he knows. Since Leonor and Don Juan speak no asides before exiting, the audience or reader also participates in this labor of hermeneutics. Could it be that Leonor's plea for Don Lope to go is a pretext for getting him out of the house, and could Don Juan's exhortation for him to stay be a veiled warning about his endangered honor? Later in the play Don Juan actually warns his friend about rumors he has heard, but at this stage of the action we do not know what Don Juan knows or suspects.

By the third act of *A secreto agravio*, Don Lope's certainty about his dishonor has reached the point that a very ambiguous remark from the king drives him into a frenzy. Even the audience is not sure of what the king means when he says: "[Q]ue en vuestra casa, aunque la empresa es alta, / podréis hacer, don Lope, mayor falta" (I, 73). We know that there have been rumors about Don Lope at court, so many that Don Juan felt obliged to warn his friend. So it is possible that the king may be trying to warn Don Lope also. The latter's predisposition to think of himself as dishonored makes him immediately place an unfavorable interpretation on these words without going through the reasoning process used in the second act. Passion has blocked out reason and goes directly to its conclusion: "¿Tan pública es ya mi afrenta, / que ha llegado a los oídos / del rey?" (I, 73). The mind has already made a judgement and the will now proceeds to act on it. The decision that reason had held in the balance for lack of conclusive evidence is now made by the overwhelming passions of jealousy and fear of dishonor.

The distortion of language extends also to dialogues. In the complex relationship between Don Juan and Don Lope we can see how the honor code's prohibition against even talking about an *agravio* puts noblemen in a double bind. At the beginning of the second act, Don Juan has a monologue which expresses the following dilemma: if he does not tell Don Lope about Don Luis de Benavides' frequent presence in the street where he lives, he is being unfaithful to the obligations of friendship, but if he does tell Don Lope, he is also being a false friend, "que al que el valor / eterno honor le previene, / quien dice que no le tiene / es quien le quita el honor" (I, 68). This is a clear statement of the recurring idea that honor or dishonor consists in the linguistic signs (*sýmbola*) of a nobleman's matrimonial honor and not necessarily in the actual state of affairs. In the ensuing dialogue with Don Lope, Don Juan finds a way of telling his friend the needed information without committing a linguistic *agravio*. He asks Don Lope what a hypothetical friend would do in such a situation, hoping that the husband will understand his speech and take it as a personal reference to himself. Don Lope does understand the message and replies, in the same hypothetical vein, that the friend should keep silent upon pain of death. His fear of dishonor makes him abandon the hypothesis for a moment and come dangerously close to speaking directly, by putting himself and Don Juan in that hypothetical situation, then placing himself alone in the same situation: "[Q]ue si yo me lo dijera, / a mí !a muerte me diera, / y soy mi mayor amigo" (I, 71). The end of this speech echoes the second act soliloquy's idea that such language should not even be spoken in solitude, for the speaker has ears to hear himself. The conditional mood has been carefully employed throughout the scene to allow each speaker to say what concerns the other, while at the same time not saying it. The words form a safe appearance under which a different and dangerous reality can be handled.

While plenty of arguments from moral theology can be adduced to condemn Don Lope and Don Gutierre, it must not be forgotten that similar arguments can be and were brought forward to defend behavior such as theirs. For example, we can hardly apply the epithets of "inordinate" and "passionate" to Alfonso X el Sabio when he says:

> [D]os yerros como eguales, matar a home et enfamarlo de mal, porque el home
> después que es mal enfamado, maguer no haya culpa, muerto es cuanto al bien
> et a la honra deste mundo: et además tal podríe ser el enfamamiento que
> mejor seríe la muerte que la vida.[18]

Theologians, jurists, and scholars of the Middle Ages through the Baroque period elaborated a theory of *sangre ilustre*.[19] Therefore when one of Calderón's characters says in *Saber del bien y del mal*, "La sangre la da el cielo," he is not only making a passionate personal statement, but also reflecting what "reason" dictated to many writers of his age.

One of the best summaries of the various attitudes toward nobility in seventeenth-century Spain has been given by Antonio Domínguez Ortiz, whose words are worth quoting extensively. He distinguishes between two main currents in the genealogical authors of the age:

> La primera [posición], ya teñida de un fuerte sabor racista con su teoría de la
> transmisión de cualidades por la sangre, ya temperada por el sentido cesarista de
> la legislación antigua que reconocía al príncipe el derecho a ennoblecer por servicios
> prestados; la segunda, de raigambre, a la vez clásico-renacentista y cristiana, que
> intentaba basar la verdadera nobleza en la virtud y el mérito, en cualidades
> personales y no heredadas. Dos concepciones que, en principio, parecen dia-
> metralmente opuestas, pero que en la práctica se mezclaron originando, en vez de
> dos nítidas escuelas de pensamiento, variedad de matices que se entrecruzan
> confusamente, cuando no palpables contradicciones en un mismo escritor. Los
> defensores de la nobleza de sangre tenían de su lado la opinión tradicional y la
> realidad cotidiana: el hijo de noble, por este mero hecho, era noble; mas no se
> atrevían a rechazar expresamente la identificación de nobleza y virtud, ni con-
> seguían explicar cómo la cualidad de noble podía hallarse en sujetos indignos
> y viles. Por su parte, los que la atribuían sólo a las cualidades personales, por
> lo regular no se atrevían a negar la influencia hereditaria (si bien hubo algunos
> que se pronunciaron con gran violencia contra la nobleza de sangre). Unos y otros
> solían convenir en una especie de eclecticismo que encubre mal la inconsistencia
> y confusión de las ideas.[20]

The only objection one might make to the above summary is the confusing impression one receives that the concept of nobility of merit and virtue, rather than that of heredity, is of Christian origin. I do not believe that such a statement would have made sense to Calderón or to his educated contemporaries. From the *Nobiliario vero* of 1492 at the beginning of the imperial period to a genealogical treatise of 1736, one could find numerous works in which sacred texts are used to support hereditary nobility. José Manuel Trelles, about fifty years *after* Calderón's death, writes:

> El orden de la Nobleza es tan antiguo como el mundo; los primeros pimpollos de la Humanidad fueron Caín y Abel. Este fue virtuoso y justo, y por eso noble; fue Caín malo, y por lo mismo plebeyo y vil; y así, en aquella primera edad del mundo sólo hubo dos linajes: buenos y malos; nobles y plebeyos; hijos de Dios e hijos de los hombres. . . . Después del Diluvio se dividió el mundo en tres órdenes; la primera, de reyes y príncipes, siendo para ella escogido Sem; la segunda, de nobles, que en servicio de estos príncipes tuviesen autoridad y gozasen excenciones y prerrogativas, para lo cual fue destinado Jafet. La tercera fue de plebeyos y viles, que no sólo sirviesen a los reyes, sino a los nobles, siéndoles en todo inferiores, y para esto fue señalado el abominable Caín [sic] y su posteridad.[21]

Thus the distinction often made between the "false" values of honor and the "true" Christian values which Calderón is advocating must be seen as partly due to the preconceptions of the critics. It involves a modern definition of the word "Christian" which reflects several centuries of European and American social change. As Domínguez Ortiz remarks, hardly any writer he has studied rejects outright the juridical or racial idea of nobility, and surely all such writers would call themselves Christians, though they may not have stated their ideas in a form as severe as that of Trelles quoted above. It must be observed that within the Catholicism of the age certain distinctions between liberal and conservative political thought can be made, for example, between the few remnants of Erasmistic ideas in Spain and the Counter-Reformation social doctrine which reacted against it. Finally, in most authors one must take into account the vacillation and inconsistency of ideas that are hidden under the oft-repeated terms *nobleza, virtud,* and *linaje.* It is generally useless, even in the *comedias* of Calderón, to try to pin the author down to a systematic, consistent position on the issue. Thus, one is perfectly free to condemn the honor code, but to do so by means of the Bible, the classics, the Church Fathers, and St. Thomas is a selective procedure and can be turned against the user.

The three parts of the foregoing analysis (hierarchy, judgement, and language) all point to a "rational" norm which the protagonists violate by following a socially imposed honor code. Yet even when this code is not present, the sexual passions can become "inordinate" in Thomist terms, as can be seen in the Herodes-Mariene relationship in *El mayor monstruo los celos.*

The important trait in Herodes' character is not honor, but love, a love for his wife which, like every other passion in the play, is expressed in hyperbolic terms in the first act.[22] He wants to immortalize his love, that is, to make his wife into an immortal goddess. His military defeats and political disappointments only distress him because they prevent him from making Mariene queen of the world. In this respect Herodes is more altruistic than the "husbands of honor." Their love for an abstract honor is stronger than their love for their wives, while Herodes is willing to sacrifice his honor for his wife's happiness. The second and third acts of *El mayor monstruo* show, however, that even the most altruistic passion, expressed with all the beauty of Baroque love poetry, can have tragic consequences. Herodes, like the "husbands of honor," breaks the traditional hierarchy of love and duty, but in this instance he does so by worshipping his wife. On one level we can say that the tragedy that ensues confirms the theological hypothesis that evil is a perversion of good through the disruption of order. It is precisely Herodes' awesome "love greater than death" which finally produces "the greatest monster in the world." He is acting like a pagan in not accepting a higher standard than his own passion. All of the characters of the play, in fact, are Judaeans or Romans. The atmosphere of the play is pre-Christian, as in some of the political plays. Direct love and hate of persons and things comprise the gamut of the characters' motives. We can attribute to most of them the final remark made about Medea in Seneca's tragedy of that name: *ubi tu veheris nullos esse deos* ("wherever you go there are no gods"). Herodes, Mariene, and Otaviano see only celestial bodies or blind fortune above them in the scheme of things, so it is natural that their relationships should be a battlefield of passions.

What has been said of love can also be said to a certain extent of jealousy. It is not jealousy itself that is harmful; it is the overwhelming jealousy that makes Herodes forget other considerations which turns out to be the "greatest monster." The Tetrarch experiences the true *Diccionario de Autoridades* definition of *celos* given earlier: the suspicion (or knowledge) that the loved one loves another or is loved by another.

Jealousy can be seen to grow out of love by virtue of the Thomistic distinction between the parts of man's sense appetite. Love, the most basic of the passions, belongs to the *concupiscibilis,* which is passively drawn to its object. It receives knowledge of its object and is attracted to it without intermediary. This is the state of things in which we find Herodes in the first act of the play, the act that writers of *comedias* normally reserved for exposition of the initial situation. At least as far as amorous rivals are concerned, no cloud has appeared on the horizon of the Tetrarch's marriage. Jealousy, on the other hand, contains elements of fear and anger, which are passions of the *irascibilis.* As has been mentioned, this part of man's appetite functions when there is an obstacle in the path of desire, adding a complication to the nature of the passion. In *El mayor monstruo,* as in other *comedias,* the complication (Otaviano's falling in love with Mariene's portrait) is set in the first act but does not have its effect until the second act, when the Tetrarch is brought captive before Otaviano. Since there is a natural progression from the *concupiscibilis* to the *irascibilis* in the face of obstacles, it is literally true that love without jealousy is like a body without a soul. The emotion of jealousy is a natural outgrowth of love and is a partial proof of love's strength. For this reason, the rise of jealousy in the minds of Calderonian characters is instantaneous upon their perception of a rival to their love. It is simply another layer of feeling added on to the already existing *concupiscentia* and will in turn be complicated by coming into conflict with other passions and thoughts. Its extreme stage will come when it turns the former love into hate, and desires the destruction of the beloved object. As the Tetrarch himself says: "¿Qué pasión ¡çielos! es ésta, / de amor hija y madre de odio? . . ." (p. 125).

The intensity of the jealousy which comes into play in the second act depends, of course, on the intensity of its cause, Herodes' love for Mariene. Given the overwhelming nature of his love, which obscured even his political ambitions, it is logical that his jealousy too should completely occupy his spirit, as he indicates in his long speech to Filipo. In the first act, his love had driven him to make treaties with both Marco Antonio and Otaviano, the rival claimants to the imperial throne. He hoped to make himself emperor for Mariene's sake. Now his jealousy leads him to an action which seems paradoxical until the inordinate character of his love is taken into consideration. He resolves to have Mariene killed secretly, since he himself is doomed to be executed and Otaviano is planning to march on Jerusalem, where Mariene resides. His rationale is the following: "[P]ues no ay amante o marido / (salgan todos a esta causa) / que no quisiera ver antes / muerta, que ajena sv dama" (p. 93).[23] If the Tetrarch proceeds to act on this impulse, it is because his mind does not listen to the restraining conscience which should remind him of other higher considerations. Like the "husbands of honor," he has lost the power of deliberation. Calderón personifies this conscience in Filipo, the old servant who acts as the Tetrarch's confidant in the first and second acts. Herodes entrusts him with the mission of having Mariene killed before Otaviano reaches Jerusalem. When he finds out what his master plans to do, Filipo tries to warn him and rebut all the arguments the Tetrarch has put forward, but he is interrupted by the guards who are coming to take Herodes to his execution. In reply to Filipo's protestations, Herodes can only say in his frenzied state: "Calla, / que sé que tienes razón; / pero no puedo escucharla" (p. 93). We have here a visible representation onstage of a precipitate passion dismissing reason by force.

The title of the play indicates to the reader that all the external objects which the characters feared would become the "greatest monster" and kill Mariene turn out to be less powerful than the interior passion of jealousy. The word *monstruo* should be taken in its original meaning of something out of the ordinary or which violates the order of nature. In Act III, Herodes describes jealousy figuratively as an animal composed of parts of many different creatures. This concept fits well with our description of Herodes' passion as an inordinate one which, not being limited by temperance, grows to an abnormal state. Although there is no character who consistently knows how he should act, the very term *monstruo* has a normative connotation.[24] And since in Thomism abnormality comes from not being connected in a right way to other beings and to the source of being, a break in the hierarchy of being produces monsters.

Such is the reasoning that a Thomistically-oriented critic would use in bringing moral judgement upon the three main characters.

On the other hand, it seems pointless to put a merely negative valuation on the tremendous forces of will that are unleashed in these dramas. On one level *El mayor monstruo* is a tragedy in the Christian sense which Parker describes, since inordinate passions bring about catastrophic results. On another level, it is a tragedy of impersonal fate in which the high-minded protagonists match their will against forces higher than themselves.[25] Part of their aristocratic ethic involves absolute desires and hatreds; they attempt to bring about results that are nearly cosmic in their implications (conquering the world, loving a woman who exists only as a portrait, suicide, etc.). The same must be said of the honor code: from a purely Christian point of view, it is blameworthy, and the tragic *dénouements* are a punishment of moral transgression on the part of all involved. From a secular aristocratic point of view (and we have no reason to suppose that Calderón did not share this point of view), the extreme actions of honor are examples of an absolute determination of will and an absolute faith in the sanctity of nobility and thus become admirable. Calderón's matrimonial plays contain an anguished dialogue between these two poles.

The fact that love and jealousy, which are purely personal passions, are pitted against political intrigue and ambition in *El mayor monstruo* makes this drama a good transition play to our next chapter, in which we will deal with reason and the passions with regard to the art of ruling a state or empire. *El mayor monstruo* cannot properly be called a political play, since the principal characters all place personal and emotional considerations above politics. It is a story of love and jealousy played out on an international scale. We will now turn our attention to a group of plays in which political and individual considerations often vie as powerful motives for the characters' actions.

3

Political Plays

Although the same range of characters appears in Calderón's political plays as in the other *comedias* under consideration, a different set of problems is emphasized in such plays as *La gran Cenobia* and *Los cabellos de Absalón*. These *comedias* will serve as examples of the Calderonian subgenre which deals with the workings of a monarchical or imperial state. The three problematic aspects (judgement, language, and hierarchy) which were used in the analysis of honor plays can now be applied to the area of statecraft, or *razón de estado*. The use of this phrase in Calderón, Gracián, Saavedra Fajardo, and other seventeenth-century authors always contains at least an implicit reference to the debates on Machiavellianism. As John Dowling has indicated, "Saavedra Fajardo used the phrase 'razón de estado' in the title of the second part of his dual treatise, *Introduction to Political Science and Statecraft of King Ferdinand the Catholic*. This expression was the most widely debated topic of the century in the art of government."[1] Dowling also states, "Europe, in bondage to the legacy of Machiavelli, was in the process of rigorously separating the sphere of politics from the sphere of morality. The process was justified by 'razón de estado,' by statecraft, by practical politics."[2] This is the guise which the problem of reason and passions assumes in relation to the political world.

First, a confusion arises in the problem of rational judgement in politics. While the husbands of the honor plays vacillate between judgements of innocence and guilt according to the passions of love or jealousy which seize them at certain moments, the political protagonists shift their standard of judgement to fit the political objectives they entertain: either personal self-aggrandizement or the good of the state. These divergent attitudes find expression in two visions of statecraft in seventeenth-century Spain: that of Gracián, particularly in *El héroe*, and that of Quevedo in *La política de Dios*.

Early in their respective treatises, both writers confirm the Thomistic doctrine that intellect is the most important human faculty. Gracián says: "Es lo mejor de lo visible el hombre, y en él el entendimiento, luego sus vitorias las mayores."[3] Quevedo explains in his first chapter how a ruler's will should follow his understanding. Yet what is meant by "understanding" is different in each case. Gracián is writing a manual on how to become a hero: a man who is esteemed and respected during his lifetime and who becomes immortally famous after his death. He therefore adds another dimension to simple understanding; he distinguishes between "fondo de juicio" and "elevación de ingenio." The former, which is a faculty involving long deliberation and patience, is dismissed in one sentence: "No abogo por el juizio, pues el habla por si bastantemente" (p. 11). It is evident that the profound sense of judgement is not especially useful to Gracián in the formation of his outstanding courtier. He rather calls upon *ingenio* to present a good front before the world.[4] This faculty is quick to respond to questions and problems with words appropriate to the occasion, with the result that the hearers of these words walk away impressed by the speaker's apparent wisdom. Since the object of Gracián's instruction is to form a man who seems great to others, *agudeza* is a great part of the political virtue of prudence. Gracián points out that Solomon's fame as a wise ruler rests primarily on his felicitous replies, such as his ingenious solution to the problem of the two women who both laid claim to the same infant: he offered to cut the baby in two and divide it equally.

Likewise, in his description of Fernando el Católico, Gracián makes astuteness equal to judgement in importance. On the one hand, this model king was "[u]n príncipe prudente, cuyo gran juicio es el contraste de todo gran caudal." On the other hand, he was "[u]n príncipe sagaz, Argos real que todo lo previene. Emulo de Janos, que mira a dos haces, de fondo inapeable, con más ensenadas que un océano."[5] Even a superficial examination of Calderón's *comedias* will encounter many examples of this ingeniousness at work, where the pressures of a dramatic situation force a character to come up with an answer based not on careful deliberation over general principles, but on the immediate need to appease two conflicting claims. Such is the case with Mariene at the end of Act II of *El mayor monstruo,* as was discussed in Chapter 1.

Quevedo's conception of *entendimiento,* on the other hand, emphasizes preestablished, eternal principles which derive from divine revelation. Each one of the counsels he gives to the monarch in *La política de Dios* is based on an incident of Christ's life as recorded in the Gospels. Christ becomes the supreme model for rulers, which should be followed unerringly, since the power to rule is given to certain men, not to be used according to their own will, but only to carry out the dictates of Providence, who anointed them as rulers. "A Vuestro cuidado, no a vuestro aluedrío, encomendó las gentes Dios nuestro Señor. . . ."[6] Quevedo's difficulty, however, is that, in making a direct correlation between Christ as king and Philip IV, he must adapt the gentle Messiah, who was humble and self-effacing on earth, to the necessarily absolutist policies of the imperial Spanish monarchy.[7] Although Quevedo's vision of politics is far more imbued with Christian ethics than Gracián's, the former is still a master of *ingenio*. His maxims presuppose a consciousness of the ruler's duty to God and of the consequent responsibility to attend to his needy subjects, that is, to practice the virtue of charity. Gracián has less to say on this subject, at least in *El político* and *El héroe*. Yet in allegorizing certain Gospel passages, Quevedo draws some metaphoric conclusions that could lead to the formation of many non-Christian traits in the ruler.

One of the Gospel episodes used in the *Política de Dios* is that of the pool of Bethesda, where at certain intervals an angel came down and stirred up the waters. The first person to bathe in the waters immediately after the angel passed would be cured of his infirmity. Jesus cures a man who had never had a chance to be cured, for he had no one to carry him down to the pool. In applying this passage to royal politics, it is not so much Jesus who is to be imitated by the king, as the angel. The merciful act of carrying the sick man to the water is to be carried out by the king's ministers, and the evil minister is the one who neglects the sick, the poor, the orphans, and widows who cannot get to the healing waters of the pool on their own. The king and only the king is to be the angel whose touch gives healing powers to the water, which represents the republic: ". . . que el Rey ha de ser Angel para dar virtud, y hazer milagros, y reboluer por su mano la piscina; pues assí tendrá virtud, y de otra mano veneno y muerte . . ." (p. 110). This sentence clearly attributes superhuman powers to the king and raises him above the common level of men, just as angels, although they too are subordinate to God, have certain privileged powers which man lacks. Yet to be an angel also implies acting as an obedient servant of God in his dealings with men. Thus a king who follows Quevedo's doctrine in this and other chapters will be a mixture of self-confident aristocrat who believes himself to be divinely elected and of humble Christian servant who knows he will be judged in the afterlife.

The problem of ruling wisely according to an ethical or religious pattern is particularly present in *La vida es sueño, El príncipe constante,* and *Los cabellos de Absalón.* The standard set for the ruler may be a general *prudencia* or wisdom, based on the transitory nature of power (Segismundo), an anointment from Jehovah (King David), or a Christian ideal (Prince Fernando). In each case, the ideal pattern is put into conflict with other motives, and ingenious thinking is required for the protagonists to extricate themselves from the predicaments they fall into on account of their less praiseworthy adversaries. It does not really help us to posit the virtue of prudence as the guiding principle of these characters, since that term acquired such a broad meaning during the course of seventeenth-century debates that it can indicate anything from the strictest adherence to Christian morality to Machiavellian tactics. "The virtue of prudence, in the concept of Spanish moralists of a political persuasion, was composed of several parts, among them moderation, knowledge of self, accommodation, dissimulation, and distrust."[8]

The analysis of the virtue of prudence, in all its ramifications, can serve as an index to the major issues debated by peninsular theorists on politics.[9] As in the case of so many terms of the age, the word *prudencia* signifies an extremely complex cluster of concepts, whose inconsistencies reveal the contours of the thought of its users. No theorist believes that a prince should be imprudent, for the authority of Aristotle backs up the contrary thesis: "prudentia est propria virtus principis."[10] The trouble starts when the nature of this virtue needs to be defined. In St. Thomas, the relation of true prudence to its sham imitators depends on the hierarchy of means and ends which form for him the structure of a human act. Prudence in the true sense must be directed toward man's true goal, the service of God, and must use means that do not contradict the end. Yet the same faculty of prudence, which St. Thomas defines as *recta ratio agibilium* ("right reason in things to be done"), can be applied to unworthy ends and become the sin of *prudentia carnis* (XXXVI, 146-48). On the other hand, improper means may be used to attain a goal, whether right or wrong, and the user of these will fall into the sins of *dolus, astutia,* and *fraus* (XXXVI, 152-58). The same cognitive faculties operate in all these cases, but their application can be wrong. It is this *applicatio ad opus* which characterizes prudence as the mediator between general principles and concrete cases. In dealing with the latter, the subject must take into consideration the circumstances, the temporal conditions which prevail at the moment of deciding upon a course of action. This part of prudence St. Thomas calls *circumspectio* and remarks that "because prudence is about individual actions . . . and these involve many factors, it may happen that a means good and suitable in the abstract becomes bad and inopportune owing to a combination of circumstances. . . . Accordingly prudence calls for circumspection in order that what is done for an end may match the circumstances of the situation" (XXXVI, 79). The idea expressed here, though it presented no problems for the well-cemented system of Thomism, opened the door for later theorists of politics to devise an art of ruling without abandoning the virtue of prudence. Maravall notes in them the following tendency: "mantienen las virtudes morales, pero reconocen y aceptan la novedad de su tiempo: el arte político."[11]

A good way to illustrate the labyrinth of statecraft in the seventeenth century is to contrast two of Saavedra Fajardo's *Empresas políticas,* in which it is apparent that the only practicable way for a prince to obey the eternal commands of virtue and worship is to pay attention to and adapt to the temporal circumstances around him and to the fluctuations of his own passions. He can only be a wise prince if he is skillful. In the *Empresa VII,* the motto reads AUGET ET MINUIT, referring to a telescope which makes things look larger or smaller than they are. According to Saavedra, it is the natural inclinations and passions which cause this distortion. Thus, reason, or more particularly *razón de estado,* must put matters into perspective, allowing the prince to judge correctly and act prudently. Note that here reason does not call for a single-minded course of action. "Si no vence y disfraza sus inclinaciones naturales, obrará siempre uniformemente, y se conocerán por ellas sus fines. . . ."12 Variation is reasonable, while uniformity indicates enslavement to the passions. I have already mentioned the tactic of Prince Fernando, who, in order to fulfill his unshakable desire for a martyr's death, changes his emotion in mid-speech and instead of pleading for mercy, tries to provoke the king's anger. In the words of Saavedra, "[u]na misma hora le ha de ver severo y benigno, justiciero y clemente, liberal y parco, según la variedad de los casos" (I, 121).

In the *Empresa XVIII,* whose motto reads A DEO, the emphasis is reversed. Following reason implies keeping one's gaze fixed on God, and change or turning away implies vice. "El príncipe que . . . volviere los ojos a las aparentes luces de bien que le representa su misma conveniencia, y no la razón, presto verá eclipsado el orbe de su poder" (I, 204). Saavedra advocates trust in Divine Providence by citing the example of Fernán Antolínez, whose place in battle was taken by an angel while he heard Mass. In this aspect the prince is to be "art-less." Clearly he must tread a razor's edge to reconcile this notion with the ever vigilant Argos advocated in *Empresa VII.*

Yet for Saavedra, Quevedo, and others the two aspects formed one rational ideal for a perfect ruler. They could not accept Machiavelli's idea that the prince must abandon moral virtue, become evil, and endanger his own salvation for the good of the state.13 They were constantly on guard against monarchy becoming tyranny; however, they were too aware of their contemporary world to believe that a king could rule successfully by following ethical precepts literally or blindly. Although, as we have seen, they often protest that Providence will guide and preserve the ruler who is inherently virtuous, they did not believe that God wanted Christian kingdoms to fall because of the prince's *naïveté.*

The important fact about the discourse of Calderón's political characters is that the "good" rulers have linguistic *agudeza* at their service just as much as the pagan, selfish, or "evil" characters. The types of thinking which would be considered sophistic for orthodox Scholasticism, since they equivocate on the meanings of words and the order of concepts, become a universal tool that can apply almost any general principle to any set of circumstances. Consider, for example, Prince Fernando's speech to the King of Fez. It is composed of a series of figurative arguments in which a medieval dialectician could find numerous faults. The point is that the speech is convincing because the reader or spectator knows that Fernando's vehement desire to glorify God is prior to the rational arguments he invents to persuade the Moorish king. The principle of *invención* is accepted on all levels of the *comedia,* that is, that the mind "finds" an argument for a specific need. Implicitly, then, the will becomes the guiding factor in discourse, no matter how much the opposite view is verbally insisted upon. Calderón's characters do not enter the scene of the action as neutral embodiments of intellect; from the very beginning they have a vital interest in what is said by other characters and what transpires. I have mentioned what the characters' vital interests consist of in the political plays, and I have suggested how *agudeza,* rather than deliberative judgement, is used to further these interests. Because *agudeza* is a verbal art, language is the principal tool for expressing and furthering the personal and political desires of each character.

Let us recall the sentence of Aristotle: "Those that are in vocal sound are signs of passions in the soul. . . ." The direct relationship implied in this doctrine is once again put into question by the use of language in politics. The love and ambition experienced by Cenobia and Semíramis, for example, are definitely "passions in the soul" which provoke speech, but the tool of language, rather than expressing an immediate emotional state, is often used for strategical purposes which ultimately aim at acquiring the beloved person or political power. Therefore, the life span of a passion such as ambition must be divided in our analysis into its active and passive components. First, a ruler must become aware of riches, power, and fame before he can desire them. This is an active mental and bodily process. Calderón represents this in *La gran Cenobia* and *Los cabellos de Absalón* by having Aureliano and Absalón accidentally come across the royal crown and scepter, which are lying on a rock (or a table in the second case) in a deserted place. Their knowledge of the essence of power and riches is extremely incomplete, as is shown in the *dénouement* of both plays, but they have at least an instinctual notion of the desirability of ruling. The effect of this knowledge on the appetite is the properly passive aspect of the passion. Aureliano, for example, sees the scepter and crown lying on a rock and goes toward them: "[P]orque un aliento nuevo, / un espíritu altivo que me inflama / el coraçón, a tanto honor me llama."[14] It is the crown and scepter which exert the influence suggested by the active verbs *inflama* and *llama,* while the speaker becomes the direct object of their action. Also, the terms *aliento* and *espíritu* both indicate an influx from the outside. After the passion is experienced, the reason and will either repress the desire or consent to it; the latter is the case of Aureliano. He is determined to crown himself, even though he recognizes in this symbol of royal power a *deidad* that demands respect. The mind becomes active again as it deliberates on the means to achieve the desired end. One of the most frequently employed means is language, which can communicate either an inner reality or a desired appearance. Aureliano seems generally incapable of using language well, since at crucial moments his immediate passions make him blurt out his true feelings and make enemies out of those who could be useful allies. In his case, it is unfortunately true that the sounds of his voice are direct tokens of the passions of his soul.

The conspirator Libio, in the same play, is a consummate artist in the use of deceptive language. He knows when to speak and when to keep silent. He embodies the virtue which Gracián calls *caudal*. The Jesuit philosopher recognizes that the highest prudence consists in directing one's actions to the highest moral good, although he refrains from developing the idea. For those who do not or cannot exercise this control, however, there is a secondary prudence, which consists in hiding the imprudent movements of the soul by carefully controlling one's own speech and bodily gestures. Thus one preserves a private terrain of thought and emotion, a *caudal* (a term which derives from the same Latin root as *capital*!), which is to be exteriorized in gestures or language only at opportune moments. The use of this tactic does not seem to be necessarily connected in Calderón's works with negative or wicked characters, but seems to be an indispensable tool of political life. It is used for purposes that may be good or evil in a larger framework, but its moral character is not in question at the moment when, because of interaction with others, a character must verbally defend a point of view, justify an action, or conceal information.

The hierarchy exhibited in these plays is above all one of political subordination. At the bottom of the scale is an invisible offstage *vulgo,* whose voices are heard outside the palaces where the nobles make their decisions. The mob acts as a single character except when it is divided into factions; then it is scornfully described by the main characters as a many-headed monster that is fickle and inconsistent. There is no doubt, however, that the murmurings of the lower classes have a great effect on the behavior of Calderonian monarchs and emperors.

The army is another large group which the rulers must take into consideration, since the rank-and-file soldiers (usually represented by offstage voices or by one or two anonymous soldiers onstage) may change their loyalty, either for patriotic or for mercenary reasons. The army is under the command of captains and generals, who swear allegiance to the ruler, but whose loyalty can also change. To maintain their allegiance, the ruler uses their desire for fame and material remuneration as well as their fear of exile or death in case of defeat. These monarchs of antiquity are also surrounded by civilian courtiers, in particular by counselors or *privados,* who advise prudently or rashly, either from ignorance or from interested motives. Often there is collusion of military with civil interests to influence the ruler in a particular direction.

At the top of the scale is the royal family, which can experience conflict within itself, either between king and queen or between royal parents and their offspring. At least two of the plays suggest a supernatural force which, through the oracle in *La gran Cenobia* and through the anointed character of King David in *Los cabellos de Absalón,* gives a religious legitimacy to the monarch's right to rule. The foregoing description constitutes a structure which rests on the use of force as well as on a voluntary submission on the part of the subjects, although the admixture of these factors varies from play to play and within individual plays.

From the viewpoint of the individual characters, the hierarchy takes on a different appearance. It becomes a ranking of desires and emotions in accordance with certain rational or passionate considerations. The honor plays have amply covered the range of sexual love, jealousy, and friendship. (*Los cabellos,* however, introduces the complication of incestuous desire.) In the political plays, ambition comes to the forefront and sets itself against love as a contender for the rational appetite of the protagonists or even the secondary characters. The desires that come into play can be summarized in the three Greek words that form the combined equivalent of the Romance word *ambitio*: *philoploutia* ("love of riches"), *philotimia* ("love of fame"), and *philarchia* ("love of rule"). The ambitious protagonists in Calderón usually experience all three of these passions in varying degrees. In some cases the desire for power seems to be innate, as in Semíramis; in others, it can be caused by love (as we have seen in the case of Herodes) or by hatred of a rival or of an existing authority. Often personal affection and social ambition start off hand in hand at the beginning of the play and end up as opposites that hinder one another. At the beginning of *La hija del aire* (Part I) Semíramis falls in love with the brave soldier who rescues her from solitude and captivity. Yet when her lover introduces her to the royal city of Niniveh, she becomes enamored of riches and power and sees her rescuer as an obstacle. Calderón's interest is generally to show how these passions react upon each other, so that he does not divide sharply between the personal and political realms; neither one is primordial in his dramatic world. We can now apply these principles to specific plays.

La gran Cenobia, for example, has six main characters, four of whom either vie for power or have power thrust upon them. At various points in the action, we will attempt to determine the relation of these changing power plays to the Thomistic idea of prudence which has been held up by many critics as a political ideal that Calderón wished to illustrate.

The first character to appear onstage is Aureliano, who begins the play dressed in the animal skins that are often used by Calderón to symbolize the natural man who is ruled by sense appetite. He has had a dream in which he saw the emperor of Rome dying and offering him his crown and scepter. After his dream monologue, he actually comes across a crown and scepter which have been left on the rocks in the forest. Aureliano thinks that they may have grown like plants out of the rocks and trees. It turns out that the former emperor had passed that way after defeat in battle and had left the crown and scepter there. Aureliano does not question his good fortune for long, but takes the royal accoutrements, drawn by an instinctive desire for the power they represent. All through the play, Aureliano is characterized by the same irreflexive passion, which makes him take things at their face value and react emotionally on a superficial understanding.

When the leader of his army, Decio, returns from the war against Cenobia and admits defeat, Aureliano immediately strips him of his position and proudly boasts that he is going to conquer Cenobia himself. His rashness is due to two factors: a lack of forethought and a lack of experience. Decio has an advantage over the new emperor in that he has already tried to vanquish the Oriental queen and knows how powerful she is in military strength and personal attractiveness.

Aureliano's rashness puts him in grave difficulties when, in the heat of battle and in flight from the pursuing enemy, he promises his crown to a masked soldier who offers to safeguard his escape; the stranger is none other than Decio. Aureliano compounds his foolishness by promising the same crown a second time to the traitor Libio, who offers to kidnap Cenobia and bring her to the emperor's tent. Later in the play, he refuses to honor his first promise, and he honors the second only to order the traitor put to death immediately afterwards. In Act III, Aureliano haughtily refuses to receive the petitions submitted by his loyal soldiers for comfortable retirements and succor for widows. Both Quevedo and Gracián condemn this fault in a ruler, the former on account of the divine commandment that we be merciful, the latter for more earthly considerations.

The one advantage afforded to Aureliano by his brute nature is that it makes him relatively insensitive to beauty and enables him to successfully resist Cenobia's charms and womanly imploring. The antagonism which he has created throughout the play, however, catches up with him and he dies at Decio's hands, having lost the support of the people and the army. He has practiced a politics of self-aggrandizement like that of Gracián's hero, but he has not learned the *razón de estado de sí mismo*, the art of governing oneself, which the Jesuit philosopher considers absolutely necessary to becoming a hero in the circumstances of monarchical and imperial states. For instance when Aureliano has heard Libio's plan to capture Cenobia, he wants to proceed to action immediately and exhorts: "Pues no hagan las razones / estorvo con sus vanas ilusiones" (I, 52). *Razones* can be taken to mean either "speech" or "reasoning" in this passage, but in either case there is a scorn for deliberation and judgement in Aureliano's words.

The emperor's antagonist is Cenobia, Queen of the Orient, who really has no more legitimate claim to her throne than Aureliano has to his, since according to the custom of her kingdom, a woman should not succeed to her husband's throne when there is a male heir, in this case a nephew, Libio. She gains favor with the nation by winning several important battles, so that when her husband Abdenato dies, she is acclaimed by the people and the army. Unlike Aureliano, she becomes a *razón de estado* unto herself and her prudence allows her to navigate the turbulent waters of politics with greater security. She takes care not to usurp her husband's functions while he is alive and to plead with him for the soldiers and courtiers who submit petitions. She combines severity and clemency in the right proportion so as to keep her followers loyal. She runs into difficulty for two reasons. First, she spares Libio's life, although she has two major opportunities to suspect that he is plotting against her. Thus a respect for her own kinsman nearly leads to her downfall, since he is responsible for her kidnapping in Act II. Second, she falls in love with the Roman general Decio, and at an important juncture at which the latter is the only soldier guarding the passage to Aureliano's tent, she does not push her troops forward ruthlessly, but respects Decio's life and his moral position of loyalty. Thus spared, Aureliano has a chance to kidnap her.

At the beginning of Act III, when Cenobia is dragged through the streets of Rome in a triumphal procession, it seems as if she has been led to political downfall by two motives that form part of every human being: family ties and erotic love. The ensuing dilemma is very typical of Calderonian thinking: the problem of two equally powerful motives, both of which have equally evil consequences. Yet Cenobia's prudence receives its reward at the end of the play; Decio assassinates Aureliano and offers to marry Cenobia and rule jointly with her. By this ingenious solution, a sort of poetic justice is enforced, since sentencing Libio to death a second time removes the male heir to the Oriental throne and Cenobia's marriage to Decio rectifies the irregularity of a woman as sole ruler. Cenobia's desire for power and her love are both satisfied in some measure. Her fortunate condition at the close of the play can be said to be a result of her intelligent balancing of two passions: ambition and love. If she had been like Aureliano, she would have steeled herself against Decio's manly charms. If she had succumbed completely to love from the beginning, she would have surrendered her kingdom's sovereignty without a fight. Calderón seems to be suggesting that there are moments when prideful resistance is the appropriate response to a situation and other moments when loving surrender is more appropriate for a female ruler.

To equate the practical-intellectual *prudentia* of Cenobia with a sort of single-minded following of abstract moral principles would make Calderón's drama infinitely less interesting than it is. Even the most innately moral of his characters are not unwilling to use all the means at their disposal to achieve a prudent goal. In Cenobia's case, she is obliged to use her natural beauty to try to melt Aureliano's heart by pretending to be in love with him. She reasons that since women are generally weak, beauty is their natural weapon. She therefore is fulfilling her natural role by trying to conquer Aureliano in this way: "Aora si que soy muger, / aora si lo he parecido; / pues con mis armas ofendo, / quando a un bárbaro pretendo / vencer con amor fingido!" (I, 70). Since Aureliano has mastered her by cunning, she must do the same to gain her freedom.

Each of the two protagonists has a male subaltern who plays a role almost as important as that of the ruler. Decio, the general of the Roman army both before and during Aureliano's reign, represents from the very beginning the rational or prudent man which Segismundo becomes at the end of his play and which Aureliano never becomes. Upon his return in Act I from a war against Cenobia, he confesses his defeats, both military and amorous, to Aureliano, who has nothing but scorn for his "cowardice." Decio is offended, but remembers that "la continua mudança / del tiempo me da esperança; / que no ay en leyes de amor, / ni tirano sin temor, / ni ofendido sin vengança" (I, 17).

Decio is certainly the character who holds the most abstract concept of duty. He subordinates both his love for Cenobia and his hatred for Aureliano to the requirements of his patriotic duty as general of the Roman army. Even when personally confronted by Cenobia on the bridge leading to Aureliano's tent, he stands firm and refuses to let her pass, combating her persuasion with the word of honor he gave to defend the emperor's person. At the beginning of Act III, although he does not repent of having been loyal, he nevertheless admits to himself that his loyalty has resulted indirectly in the capture of the woman he loves: "[P]ues la ventaja que muestra / en este triunfo Aureliano, / es que en sus fortunas tengan / él un leal que le guarde, / y ella un traidor que la venda" (I, 62). Once again we see the typically Calderonian contrast between the viewpoint of a particular moment at which loyalty seems a mistake and that of the play as a whole from which it appears that Decio's loyalty is ultimately instrumental in making him emperor. The people trust him because of his refusal to surrender to Cenobia in previous battles. In other words, in spite of his final act of regicide, Decio is loyal to Rome in the abstract and ends up satisfying his love interest as well.

Decio is finally determined to commit regicide by the sight of Cenobia imploring Aureliano and feigning love for him. Thus the final emotional jolt that stirs Decio to action is accidental, since he is reacting to a situation he does not understand and his arrival onstage at that moment is contingent and unmotivated. No matter that shortly thereafter Cenobia explains the real situation to him, thus resolving their lovers' quarrel. Calderón has seen fit to use a dramatic twist, which is typical of the Lopesque style of *comedia,* to detonate the growing thoughts and emotions of indignation against Aureliano that have built up in several characters in Acts II and III. Again the Scholastic doctrine of reason and passions is superseded by a more modern psychological representation. By the middle of Act III, all the main characters (Decio, Astrea, Cenobia), as well as the populace, are aware that Aureliano is a tyrant and that he deserves to be deposed for his total disregard of rights and laws. None of the above-mentioned parties seems willing to actually go against him until Decio's passionate moment of jealousy, however unfounded that jealousy may be. Just like the "husbands of honor," this character requires a "last straw" to serve as a catalyst for an action that in this case appears reasonable and laudable to the other characters. It is peculiar that the more personal motive of jealousy is a stronger force than military or political revenge; Decio makes his resolution in these terms: "[M]uera un fiero Emperador; / no porque ofendió mi honor, / no porque triunfó de ti; / porque me dio zelos sí, / que ya es agravio mayor" (I, 74). In matters of love, Decio slips back into the mode of a natural man to whom the immediate sensible reality is more efficacious than abstract ideas, although it so happens in this case that jealousy leads to a praiseworthy action. There are other passages in the play which suggest that love toward the opposite sex is an almost invincible passion that must be given its due for a person to be fully human. The real *hombre-fiera* of the play, Aureliano, is surprisingly the one who resists Cenobia's charms, although he is forced to admit at one point: "[S]in duda que no advirtió / tal belleza, el que pensó / que era libre el alvedrío" (I, 71).

Decio's opposite is Libio, the traitor, who, instead of being activated by a wide range of human motives, has only one facet to his character, the ambition to rule. His claim to the throne is legitimate in that as the nephew of the old king, he is the closest male heir and should have precedence over Cenobia. She is superior to him, however, in popularity and military prowess, so Libio resorts to treachery in order to obtain the throne. He and his accomplice, Irene, assassinate Abdenato by a secret poison, hoping that the murder will be blamed on Cenobia, but the plan backfires. After Abdenato's death, Cenobia is acclaimed queen and Libio is completely passed over. His second strategy is to offer his services to Aureliano as kidnapper of Cenobia. He carries out this plan successfully, but the reward he expects from Aureliano becomes a punishment. The latter orders Libio put to death, according to the famous logic of Segismundo that once the treachery is committed, the traitor is no longer needed and, if allowed to continue in favor, might commit treachery against the one who had employed his services.[15] Luckily for Libio, Irene has a ring with the imperial seal which Aureliano had given to the traitor, and it enables her to rescue her accomplice from the death sentence. Libio's final attempt at power is to murder Aureliano, which occurs coincidentally at the very moment when Decio attempts the same act. In the final scene, both the loyal Roman and the treacherous Oriental attempt at different moments to kill Aureliano, but each is forced to hide because the other arrives. Two patterns of behavior, as morally different as night and day, end with the same act, thus relativizing the sharp distinctions that moral theologians liked to make between the consequences of virtue and vice. Decio is the one who finds the opportune moment and commits the act, is proclaimed emperor, and repeats Aureliano's action at the end of Act II by once again ordering the traitor put to death. This time there is no escape for Libio.

In fact, both Libio and Decio, when they try to stab the emperor, hurl the same four epithets at him: *bárbaro, tirano, soberbio,* and *cruel.*

This symmetry either is due to a love of exact parallelisms on Calderón's part or shows that such value judgements tend to lose their sharp contours in the arena of royal politics, a fact which becomes clear in the final scene. Decio orders Libio put to death, presumably for having kidnapped Cenobia, Decio's future wife. For this act, he deserves the designation of *traidor*. Libio, on the other hand, calls Aureliano *cruel* because Aureliano deprived him of the reward he had been promised in return for the kidnapping. Although Decio claims to be executing Libio and Irene for their crimes, we know that another fundamental motivation is to assure his life and Cenobia's against further assassination attempts.

The entirety of *La gran Cenobia*, then, presents a veritable labyrinth of political and personal means and ends. This, of course, can be said of most of Calderón's dramas of royalty, but what stands out here is the character of Decio. We may venture to suggest that he turns out to be the most "positive" character precisely because of his sensitivity to several opposing demands on his emotions, his judgements, and his actions.[16] His prudence consists in being a middle term between the passion-bound Aureliano and the coldly calculating Libio. He contains the one grain of madness, in the form of jealousy, that puts a rational prudence into motion, a prudence which by intellectual considerations alone might have remained forever deliberating and never have acted. Without a doubt, Calderón has repeated in *La gran Cenobia* his characteristic parallelism of virtuous characters and treacherous characters with the final triumph of the former. Yet the virtuous man's triumph here is not a merely providential act, as in certain other plays. It depends also on a strong will which is determined to obtain whatever it wills, whether the object be proper or improper according to classical ethics.[17]

In more precise terms, what Calderón does in the case of a character like Decio is not so much to make the strong will impervious to ethical concerns. On the contrary, almost every impulse of his behavior is justified by a general precept. Calderón rather defies his audience or readers to discover one infallible moral solution to the character's dilemma, one that would not harm some vital interest or break some moral law. Thus when a reader states that a character like Decio acted well in a certain situation or should have acted in accordance with some command, he often ends up showing the one-sidedness of his own thinking, which amounts to nothing less than what we have described as passion. Surely this has never been more the case in Calderonian studies than in the polemic over Segismundo's treatment of the "rebel soldier" in Act III of *La vida es sueño*. I have not the slightest intention here of trying to contribute to a solution to the problem. I would only like to point out briefly how the elements that come into play in this scene illustrate the central problem of this study.

The best statement I have read on this issue comes from Alan Paterson:

... while some have seen the final Segismundo as a type of Stoic-Christian hero, who maintains order and banishes the dark world of unreason, others have recognised him as a tyrant who renews a cycle of injustice in the name of political expediency. In readings as diverse as these there is a lesson: ambiguity is all. To weight interpretation toward a systematic belief, providential or Machiavellian, is to upset the quivering balance of uncertainty.[18]

Reason makes this very demand on Calderonian protagonists. They must maintain that "quivering balance" of opposing demands, and critics of these plays must make the same demand on themselves. The critics in this case are divided between attributing Segismundo's action to "imparcialidad judicial" or "pragmatismo interesado."[19] The first motive, which implies that the soldier has committed treason against Basilio, his natural lord, by freeing Segismundo from the tower, contains elements of both reason and passion. It can be shown that the soldier has a retributive debt to pay for his act of treason in order for justice to be upheld. Segismundo's recent acquisition of power, however, blinds him to the fact that he has reaped the fruits of this treason and has led a revolt against his father. Despite the New Testament warning, he has, in a sense, not seen the beam in his own eye while trying to remove a mote from his neighbor's eye, or if he is conscious of this hypocrisy, he does not let it show through in these public acts. Another curious interpretation of Segismundo's wisdom and justice is given by Barry W. Ife:

El mandamiento a la torre, dado en los términos en los que se da, es tanto un premio como un castigo porque la verdadera respuesta al "¿qué me darás?" del soldado es "una oportunidad," una ocasión para sacar el mismo provecho de la experiencia en la prisión que había sacado Segismundo.[20]

The quotation given does not do justice to the full argumentation provided by the author, yet here too we can see a passionate underside to Segismundo's action. In giving the soldier this "opportunity" to purify his soul, isn't Segismundo arrogating to himself the function of God's providence, since this is not an invitation but an imprisonment? Thus, on one side, we can see an excess of expansive emotions (love of power, pride) at work in this decision. To be impartially just in such a complex political situation does not require an emotionless condition, but rather a high degree of self-confidence (even an excessive degree, as some might claim).

Another requirement of the situation is quick thinking, since time is of the essence in producing an impact on an audience, both for Calderón, who is concerned with producing *admiración* in his audience, and for Segismundo, who is trying to make an impressive start as a ruler by awing his audience of courtiers. Readers who try to interpret the rebel soldier problem are usually exasperated by the laconic treatment given to it by Calderón (and Segismundo), a total of about thirteen lines from the soldier's petition to the awed exclamations of Basilio, Astolfo, and Rosaura. Yet what is kept in silence here is necessarily part of the political strategy. Segismundo answers the soldier's question, "¿Qué me darás?", with two words, "la torre," in which we can find a complex conceptual meaning. The brevity and apparent justice of the initial answer, giving a tower for a tower, must be seen as calculated to produce a certain effect. In comparing this passage with other laconic replies like it, it seems more likely to me that Calderón did not expect the actor playing Segismundo to pause before these words or, at least, not to seem to deliberate long over them. His explanation of the words "la torre" is also succinct and unsatisfactory, yet the exclamations of the other characters show what seems to be a full comprehension and approval of his action. Of course, we can always attribute these lines to a desire to please the new ruler who has just granted Basilio, Astolfo, and Rosaura unexpected favors. "BASILIO: Tu ingenio a todos admira. / ASTOLFO: ¡Qué condición tan mudada! / ROSAURA: ¡Qué discreto y qué prudente!"[21]

The whole last scene of the play is performed in a public context, both because of the presence of the traditional *acompañamiento* onstage and because of the importance of these moments for the future of the Polish kingdom. There is no opportunity for asides or soliloquies, so we interpret the characters' sincerity at our own risk. Above all, we would feel much surer of Segismundo's last speech about his new-found wisdom if he had not just dealt with the rebel soldier in such a way, or if he were to speak an aside to the audience. This, however, would ruin the authoritative character of the scene, for if too much time is allowed to elapse after the initial moment of surprise, the *admiración*, which is a momentary paralysis of the mental powers, may wear off and reason may begin to dig beneath the apparently just proclamation.

Even if Segismundo's sentence is seen as due to pure, self-interested pragmatism, there is still an interplay of reason and passions to be observed in it. Segismundo reasons that the soldier who has once committed treason against the Polish crown may do so again. After his first act of treason, the soldier is not only not needed ("... el traidor no es menester / siendo la traición pasada. . . .") but is dangerous to allow in the palace. His thought may be attributed to true prudence or to what St. Thomas calls *prudentia carnis,* depending on the value one places on the end Segismundo is trying to achieve: to prevent another from occupying his throne. Yet various patterns of practical reason could demonstrate that the means are well chosen and necessary. For a Machiavellian, there is no higher end, so that Segismundo's action is entirely reasonable, but from another point of view we can see fear in the new king, a fear which does not trust either God or the subjects of the kingdom. As a contrasting example, we will see Eraclio of *En la vida todo es verdad y todo mentira* in Chapter 4, who has no fear for his political future and says of Providence, "él volverá por su causa." This is a concise version of the variously stated doctrine of classical, medieval, and Renaissance ethics and constitutes an important building block of seventeenth-century Spanish political writings, especially as regards their anti-Machiavellian attacks. The virtuous prince has nothing to fear, for God reigns and will maintain him on the throne. If he, being virtuous, is deposed, then Providence must have some inscrutable end in view in allowing such an event to occur.

Returning to Segismundo's case, it must be remembered that the soldier's original motivation had been to prevent Basilio from putting a foreign prince on the throne and to restore Segismundo, the natural heir, to his rightful position. If indeed Segismundo fears a repeat of the soldier's actions, he is revealing his intention to rule tyrannically, perhaps even more so than his father. Thus the brilliant calculator, whose *ingenio* amazes the courtiers, may be driven by an animal passion. If, as Machiavelli says, the prince should play both beast and man, then this is a bestial moment for Segismundo, in that he is acting like an animal at bay, or, at least, afraid of being cornered in the future. To further complicate matters, we may mention T. E. May's contention that this very fear leads Segismundo to choose the *wrong* means to put the soldier out of commission. A true Machiavellian, he argues, would have pardoned the soldier and given him employment at court where the royal spies could keep an eye on him, perhaps to be followed by the soldier's "mysterious" demise by a discretely administered poison.[22]

In contrast to characters like Decio and Segismundo who end the *comedia* on a triumphant note, let us examine the figure of King David in *Los cabellos de Absalón*: the multitudinous demands on his affection and judgement bring him to the brink of destruction. The process of this deterioration has been described by Gwynne Edwards as one of succumbing to "weakness" and "imperfection," an "indulgence" of his sons' faults.[23] The description of the factors involved in David's predicament is accurate, but there is a tendency to use judgemental terms like those just quoted with an inadequately explained conception of what "perfection," "strength," and "self-control" would mean in the dramatic world of this play, since so few characters exhibit these qualities. Edwards states that the Calderonian characters, like all human beings under the dramatist's "essentially Christian view of life," are "endowed with reason . . . to help [them] avoid those pitfalls into which [their] human imperfections may lead [them]. . . ."[24] When reason fails to prevail, the characters experience tragic consequences. The term "reason," however, is taken at face value and passion is taken as its opposite. The latter is equated with natural tendencies, such as ambition, filial love, sexual desires, etc., which go against reason when indulged, but which prevent us from judging the character too harshly, thus fulfilling the compassionate side of Aristotle's catharsis. The close affiliation of Edwards' study with Parker's definition of Calderonian tragedy leads us to assume that there is a metaphysic of nature and grace at work in his conclusions and that there is a "perfection" outside the play's action, to which the character's imperfection can be compared. The ideal pattern to which King David should have conformed is left unspecified, except that it implies following "reason."[25] But we have already begun to see that reason is just as much a political tool as deception or force, since it always starts from certain unquestioned presuppositions.

One of David's loyal followers, Joab, boasts: "Yo siempre / la razón, señor, defiendo." In this case reason means loyalty to a specific king whom Joab believes to have been anointed by God. On the other hand, Aquitofel, one of the followers of Absalón in his attempt to overthrow his father, uses *razón* in a different context: "¿No sabes cuán pocas veces / la dura razón de Estado / con la religión conviene?"[26] Here Aquitofel's reason presupposes that attainment and preservation of power is the ultimate good. Still another definition is given by the same Joab who claimed to defend reason in general: "La justa razón de Estado / no se reduce a preceptos / de amor . . ." (p. 137). He speaks these words just before piercing Absalón's body with three lances, although his divinely appointed leader David had commanded him to bring Absalón back alive. He appeals to an instinctive feeling of justice which dictates that he kill the rebellious son of his king. His "reasons of state" are worked out as follows: "Menos una vida importa, / aun de un príncipe heredero, / que la común quietud / de la restante del reino" (p. 137). When King David finds out about Absalón's death, Joab regrets his action and asks for pardon. In the long run, his hurling of the lances was an act of passion, not of reason, although he was able to give a logical justification for his action at the time of performing it. Just as *razón* is almost always used in the singular, though there are many forms of it operating in the play, so the concept of *justicia*. Aquitofel remarks ironically: "Dices bien, si consideras / que la justicia, una y sola, / dos no se ve que la tengan; / y así, de cualquiera causa / haber un quejoso es fuerza / por lo menos" (pp. 111-12). There is a conceptual play here between the existence of *one* justice because it is the same for all, i.e., universal, and the existence of *one* justice as *my* particular sense of it, which excludes everyone else. In this sense no two people can receive justice, since each one has a different idea of what would be just in a particular case.

The splintering of reason and its correlate justice into various particular, mutually exclusive reasons is reflected in the predicament of the king. Not only is he subject to demands from the outside, which all claim to be reasonable and just, but his inner thoughts are divided between conflicting instincts and emotions. In two separate instances he must choose between the punishment due to one of his sons and the pardon he would like to grant. In both cases he opts for pardon and suffers tragic consequences. Unlike Decio, who is able to be faithful to several duties at the same time through shrewd thinking, David is faced twice with an either-or situation. It is appropriate that Tamar, in her speech asking David to punish her incestuous seducer Amón, should refer to Abraham's willingness to sacrifice Isaac, which is perhaps the supreme

Old Testament example of a father faced with a strenuous, implacable choice (p. 76).[27]

By comparing the titles of Tirso de Molina's original play, *La venganza de Tamar,* and Calderón's reworking, *Los cabellos de Absalón,* we see that there are two basic issues interwoven in the final plot: incest and political ambition. These two are so closely combined that in Act II they culminate in one unified rebellion against David. There are three principal characters who oppose David for three different reasons: Absalón has an ambitious and vain personality disposition (or *natural* in Renaissance terminology). He manifests this nature from his first appearance onstage until his death in the last scene. Amón is a loyal son of the king until he becomes a slave to the passion of incestuous desire, which automatically puts him at odds with the moral code which his father is bound to uphold. Tamar, finally, becomes justifiably defiant when the king is unwilling to avenge her dishonor at Amón's hands. Thus Calderón illustrates three motives for disloyalty: an innate tendency, a mental sickness that overcomes the subject, and a reaction to injustice on the part of the ruler.

David's handling of the first crisis, that is, his unwillingness to punish Amón, fans the flame of ambition in Absalón and makes him join forces with Tamar. Thus when the second crisis occurs (the rebellion), David is faced with a compound defiance, a sort of filial disobedience raised to the second power. In a series of dramatic crescendos and diminuendos, the incest theme runs its course, and as it dies out with the assassination of Amón, it gives way to an intensification of the theme of ambition. Absalón's killing of his brother, which constituted the end of Tirso's play, possesses additional value in Calderón's *comedia,* since it initiates a series of acts of defiance that will culminate in the rebellion. Each new event adds a layer of new feeling to David's emotional condition, which begins on a triumphant note and ends in extreme sadness.

The key to David's suffering in the play is to be found in the opening scene, in which he exclaims affectionately to his children: "Queridas prendas mías, / báculos vivos de mis luengos días, / dadme todos los brazos" (p. 37). The passage contains three expressions, "prendas mías," "báculos vivos," and "luengos días," which prefigure the main action of the play and which indicate at the outset that the main cause of the dramatic conflict is David's age. Thus the problem of "imperfection" and "weakness" which we may see in David's character cannot be divorced from that of old age vs. youth. The first phrase, "prendas mías," points out David's emotional dependence on his children and his unwillingness to part with any of them. He values them above all else, as shown by his remark after the final military victory in which Absalón dies: "Toda la victoria diera / de una vida sola en precio . . ." (p. 139). The second phrase, "báculos vivos," symbolizes his political dependence on his children; he has appointed Amón, the firstborn, as his successor, but Amón's criminal act weakens this line of succession and motivates another son, Absalón, who in spite of being a "báculo" to his father is still "vivo" and has a will of his own, to rebel against the unjust situation. The final phrase, "luengos días," indicates David's condition at the beginning of the play: his physical and mental decrepitude. There has been weakening of certain emotions of the *irascibilis* in him; he has attained the height of his military and political career; the emotions of desire, hope, and despair, which refer to a future good, affect him little, since he is most concerned with preserving the good he has, i.e., his kingdom and his children. He begins the play in a state of joy, which is the enjoyment of a present good, in this triumphant return to Jerusalem where his children are waiting. The rivalries and crimes which threaten and ultimately destroy this happy state cause fear in him as they approach and sadness when they actually occur. Very seldom do we find David in anger, the passion that gives the *irascibilis* its name. Still less do we find *audacia,* which confronts an imminent evil and tries to halt its realization. Most of his emotional states belong to the *concupiscibilis,* except fear, which is a flight from an evil which is difficult to overcome. The sons of David, on the other hand, are in the prime of life and are full of the passions of the *irascibilis.* Absalón, for example, has a great desire and hope to reign. He is not lacking in daring to carry his project through difficulties. Also, he experiences anger when his ambition is thwarted. He specifically draws attention to the age difference when he challenges his father in battle: "Decid a David, mi padre, / . . . que si se acuerda de cuando / joven era, y en su pecho / duran algunas reliquias / de aquel pasado ardimiento, / que no se esconda de mí . . ." (p. 135). The words "pasado ardimiento" should be taken literally, for according to the physiology of the time, old age involved an actual cooling of the blood, which constituted the bodily counterpart of the weakening of the *irascibilis* in the emotions.

It is intriguing that, at various times, David, and Salomón, his only completely loyal son, are termed wise and prudent, while the ambitious Absalón is classified as rash and "mal aconsejado." This distinction raises the following problem: What is the relationship between wisdom and courage? Is the latter based on confidence in the justice of one's cause or is wisdom on the other hand a euphemism used to hide a lack of courage? Two lines from the play, spoken by one follower of Absalón and one of David, express the issue straightforwardly: "AQUITOFEL: Siempre el temor fue muy cuerdo. / JOAB: Antes, siempre la cordura / fue muy valiente" (p. 63). Their interchange raises an issue which is vital throughout the play, especially when the reader or spectator witnesses David, the anointed king of Israel, fleeing for his life and even admitting that his "justice" is ineffective. When Semey mutters against him: " ¡Mal haya quien a padecer nos trujo!", David does not reproach him and does not even offer resistance when the former angrily tries to throw a stone at him. Until the final scene of the play, it seems as if it were true of this rebellion that, as Joab says, "en comunidades, siempre / el traidor es el vencido / y el leal es el que vence" (p. 123).

In the end, David's side triumphs; several characters affirm that Absalón's accident is a punishment from God. The reader need not accept this affirmation as putting a seal of finality on the play. For the seventeenth-century audiences, the force of religious tradition would have made it a matter of course to interpret the ending in this way. Calderón was obliged by his sacred source material to make David victorious, but the final words of the play show that it is a hollow victory, for David wishes he could have saved his son's life rather than the kingdom. So even in the final speech, the conflicts of two desires (and two reasons) continue to operate: the love and duty of a father versus the onerous *razón de estado*. We are reminded of the proverblike title of Rojas Zorrilla's play *No hay ser padre siendo rey*. In Calderón's drama, it is too late for a solution of the type presented there, since passion, in the person of Joab, has hurled three lances into Absalón's body before his hair can be extricated from the boughs of the tree which ends up serving as his gallows. Yet the real interest of the dramatic action does not lie in the perfunctory affirmations of divine justice in the last scene, but rather in the conflicts of reason and passions that lead to the *dénouement,* and in these factors the question of what should have been done is hard to resolve. Different answers can be arrived at by concentrating first on the opinions expressed by various characters and then on the objective action which unfolds before our eyes.

Having observed the transformations of motifs in several political plays, we can begin to pick out certain recurring themes that we have seen in embryonic form in the matrimonial plays and which will be dealt with deliberately and more abstractly in the philosophical plays. The contrast of man and woman, for example, is dealt with in *A secreto agravio* almost completely in terms of the supposed infidelity which unifies the plot. Any comments on womanly nature are confined to the aspect of marital fidelity and honor. As we move on to *La gran Cenobia* and *La hija del aire,* the contrast between the sexes is drawn more consciously and certain abstract ideas on the nature and normal functions of each sex are implied (although these are pointed out by portraying women who break the mold). In the next chapter, the male-female relationship will not only be explored as an expression of certain facets of human nature, but also as a symbolic reference to cosmic notions, since the man becomes a *pequeño mundo* (microcosm) and the woman a *pequeño cielo.*

The sexual motif loses its autonomy in the philosophical plays and will be interwoven, in an often complex way, with other motifs which have also undergone a process of abstraction: youth vs. age, strength vs. weakness, force vs. the seduction of beauty, free will vs. determinism, brute nature vs. civilization, ambition vs. *desengaño,* and the pen vs. the sword. It remains to be shown how these motifs are connected to our major theme of reason and the passions.

4

Philosophical Plays

In one sense it is artificial to make a distinction between the "philosophical plays" of Calderón and his other *comedias,* since it has been pointed out many times that, in general, the Calderonian style is in itself much more philosophical than that of Lope. If we make such a distinction in the following pages, it is one between plays in which highly abstract reasoning has a subordinate function, as in the honor plays, and those in which the whole action of the play becomes a way of philosophizing. In the honor plays, the soliloquies and dialogues are studded with aphorisms and general observations, but the speeches as a whole deal with the particular issue of conjugal honor. In a play like *La estatua de Prometeo,* the reader's attention is constantly being brought back to the universal theme. We approach here something like a secular version of an *auto sacramental,* especially in the mythological plays, where allegory is the principal literary device employed.

The philosophical theme which interests us for the purposes of this study is that of knowledge. The themes we have developed up to this point receive a much more abstract slant in *En la vida todo es verdad y todo mentira* and *La estatua de Prometeo.*

The problem of youth vs. age is transformed into that of experience and knowledge, for an old man is supposedly wiser than a young man because he has lived more years. Thus the old man Astolfo in *En la vida,* who knows the world, is contrasted with his wards Eraclio and Leonido, who experience nothing but wonder in the face of a world they do not know. Yet their innate reasoning faculty leads them to correct conclusions and sometimes the old man is shown up by the youths. These scenes can be seen as a dramatic representation of the relative value of innate knowledge and experience, which are symbolized countless times in Calderón by the contrast between brute nature and civilized human nature. Prometeo in *La estatua* makes a distinction between "la lógica natural" and "la clara lumbre pura de la enseñanza." In another instance, both Eraclio and Leonido have a partial idea of what a woman is like from the information supplied to them by Astolfo. In Eraclio's case, the idea is positive; to Leonido, a woman must be a terrible creature.

Only Astolfo, who has actually had contact with women, has the complete picture and teaches them that they are both right since "es cualquiera mujer pintura a dos visos."

Moreover, we cannot separate the problem of knowledge from that of *desengaño,* which is itself symbolized by old age in many texts. As Góngora puts it in the *Soledad primera,* in reference to the nuptial couple's future tomb: "cuya lámina cifre desengaños, / que en letras pocas lean muchos años."[1] Experience, which is a necessary component in education for life in the world, brings many characters up against the limits of their actions or against the consequences of certain forms of action. This information could not have been reasoned out beforehand; it could only be obtained through experience. The expression *tocar la ocasión* is often used to indicate such a moment of practical discovery which changes the hypothetical expectations that the character had formed in the intellect. These expectations are often incarnated in an inexperienced youth, while the *desengaño* is found in an old character or in the same youthful character after many years have passed (e.g., Chato in *La hija del aire,* Part II). Sor Juana Inés de la Cruz expresses the same concept in an oxymoron when she speaks of hope which must eventually be disappointed: "senectud lozana, decrépito verdor imaginado."[2]

Thus there is ample treatment in the philosophical *comedias* of the ways in which knowledge is acquired and of the factors which impede its acquisition. Calderón, however, also addresses himself to the larger question of the value of knowledge and reason, especially in comparison with direct action and violence. The mythological drama *La estatua de Prometeo* takes up this question. It deals on an allegorical plane with the famous debate on arms vs. letters.[3] Without doing a gross injustice to the play, one can see it as a Baroque reinforcement of the intellectualist doctrine which we outlined at the beginning of this study. In very few other Calderonian plays are the two sides of an issue so seemingly clear: on the one hand we have Prometeo, whose name in Greek means "forethought" and who represents more or less the contemplative life and the life of learning, and on the other hand, Epimeteo, whose name means "afterthought" and who represents the active life. Each of these characters has the protection of a goddess: Minerva, goddess of wisdom, takes Prometeo's part, while Palas, goddess of war, aids Epimeteo. Prometeo spends his time immersed in "la paz de la lectura," while his brother spends his hunting animals, which symbolize his predominantly nonrational nature. In the final scenes, as in those of *Los cabellos,* one side is triumphant and is apotheosized: Prometeo is pardoned by the gods who threatened to punish him, and as a reward he receives the hand of Pandora in marriage. This finale confirms Prometeo's statement in his initial speech: "[C]uanto a la noble / naturaleza la injuria / quien la racional aplica / al comercio de la bruta. . . ."[4] The whole is an extended praising of knowledge and of those who bring knowledge to mankind, since it can be said that they give "voz al barro, y luz al alma" (p. 32), an attribute which is almost godlike in its resemblance to the creator. Boccaccio, in a passage referring to Prometeo, says that he who changes natural men into civil men through education almost re-creates them (*eos . . . quasi de novo cre[a]t*).[5] To most critics of the play, it has seemed that Calderón followed St. Thomas' division between the contemplative and the active life as well as his placement of contemplation as a higher activity than that of the worldly *homo faber*.[6] Certain reservations must be stated with regard to such an interpretation.

First, even though we may see Prometeo and Epimeteo as opposites from beginning to end, it must be remembered that they are twin brothers, a fact which later in his life arouses Prometeo's curiosity about natural causes: "Opuestos crecimos, no / en la voluntad, que anuda / nuestros corazones, pero / en la inclinación, que muda / los genios . . ." (p. 5). The two brothers exhibit a normal brotherly love for each other and they recognize each other's talents, but their inclinations are contrary. Prometeo has devoted himself to the study of causes and effects, since the circumstances surrounding his own birth made him wonder:

> [Q]ue una
> estrella, en un mismo instante,
> un mismo horóscopo, infunda
> dos afectos tan contrarios,
> con ansia de ver si apura
> el ingenio, que una causa
> varios efectos produzca,
> me di a la especulación
> de causas y efectos, suma
> dificultad, en que toda
> la filosofía se funda.
>
> (p. 5)

According to astrological science, two babies born under the same configuration of stars should have the same character, yet in this case, the rule fails.

It is true that in Prometeo's first monologue he comes out for learning as man's highest faculty: "Este anhelo de saber, / que es el que al hombre le ilustra / más que otro alguno . . . me movió en joven edad / a dejar la patria en busca / de maestros . . ." (p. 5). This, however, is the point of view of one character, who is only one half of a set of twins. Although he may be the most important character, he is not complete without his brother, who possesses the high-spiritedness that is portrayed in the character of Absalón. The same can be said of the pair of goddesses, Palas and Minerva; in traditional mythology, they are the same goddess, whereas here the divinity is split in two. Palas becomes exclusively the goddess of war, while Minerva represents wisdom. They too are twin daughters (of Jupiter and Latona) and once again they are equal in merits and accomplishments: "En valor y en hermosura, / en majestad y grandeza / nacimos las dos conformes . . ." (p. 16). Yet they have opposite inclinations, and for this reason Minerva and her sister were supposed by some to be one and the same person.

The other obstacle to Prometeo's superiority is that Epimeteo many times engages in the same sort of activity as his brother. For instance, Epimeteo admires and worships the statue of Minerva just as much as does his brother, but with the difference that Prometeo saw the image of the goddess first in his mind and thereupon made a statue to capture this vision in a material figure, whereas Epimeteo is enamored directly of the lifeless statue. There is an intellectualist symbolism in these actions, but nevertheless both brothers are enamored of the same woman in one form or another. In fact, Epimeteo is the one who courts the statue most consistently and assiduously, since his forceful character makes him pursue her even though she abhors him. Yet Prometeo, for all his *pro-videntia,* undergoes a period of confusion in which Discordia's trickery clouds his mind and he begins to hate his own creation, although she amorously pursues her creator. Thus Calderón repeats, on a symbolic plane, the dramatic device of the frustrated amorous triangle which Sor Juana describes in a sonnet: "Al que ingrato me deja, busco amante; al que amante me sigue, dejo ingrata. . . ." There is something to be said for Epimeteo's role as constant lover, who welcomes even vituperation from his beloved's lips. He is willing to carry out the execution of Prometeo and Pandora, yet only does so for reasons of jealousy that have been partially justified in other plays in characters like Herodes and Decio. In a similar vein, Epimeteo challenges the audience to consider whether they would act differently in his place: "Si alguno culpa . . . ame aborrecido y tenga / celos, y verá que son / celos y aborrecimiento / quien los acusa, y no yo" (p. 63). Instead of saying that Epimeteo symbolizes brute nature in the sense of arbitrary cruelty or indifference, it would be more correct to say that he represents the force of will, which actually accomplishes more concrete ends in the world than the intellect alone.

Furthermore, the intellectual is often forced to take action when circumstances require it. When a wild beast threatens to destroy the valley of the Caucasus, Prometeo follows his brother's example by closing up his study cave and taking up the bow and arrow. Therefore Valbuena Briones' declaration seems to overstate the case somewhat: "La guerra civil—o sea la discordia interior—nace cuando los pensadores o intelectuales no pueden contener a los militares u hombres de acción."[7]

In this and other respects, the allegorical vehicle which Calderón has adopted to embody the theme of letters vs. arms or knowledge vs. force, while showing the thesis clearly, also escapes from the thesis and shows us certain ideas, as it were, behind Calderón's back (or at least behind the back of the literally minded reader). First, the choice of a goddess and later of a beautiful woman to represent knowledge tends in itself to undermine the intellectualist hypothesis. When Prometeo, locked away in his cave for many years, has a recurring vision of Minerva, he describes it as a form of madness, just as any Renaissance love poet would describe the vision of his beloved in dreams. One of Prometeo's reasons for making the statue is to give vent to his madness, to somehow follow his obsession as far as it will lead him, so he can be rid of its power over him: "[P]ero como a la locura / es tal vez el complacerla / cierto género de cura, / complacer quise a la mía, / siguiendo su tema en una / estatua . . ." (p. 7). He categorizes his vision as a *tema*, a term which is also used to describe the mental wanderings of Don Quijote and "el licenciado Vidriera." Madness is perhaps the supreme example of a passion in the Thomistic sense of one's will being overcome by an image or sense object. So even at the outset Prometeo is not a man who is in control of all his mental functions.

If the statue is a product of madness, it is also an object of religion. When Prometeo comes out of his cave and issues a call to all the inhabitants of the Caucasus to gather around him, it is in order to show them the statue and have them worship it. The statue is, after all, that of a goddess and it is Prometeo's hope that its beauty will cause wonder (*admiración*) in the inhabitants and in his brother. From Prometeo's opening monologue we learn that after studying in various lands, he returned to his homeland and tried to impart his knowledge to the inhabitants, but they would not receive the laws by which he sought to impose a *político gobierno*. Now they seem willing enough to accept the new religion he proposes to them. So these half brutes, half humans are brought under control not by rational argument, but by art and religion, which are inseparable, since religion depends on aesthetic effects for its impact on ignorant people. Therefore Epimeteo advises his brother not to keep the statue exposed to public view until he and the people have finished building the temple where she is to be housed, for if she is constantly in view, the inhabitants will begin to take her for granted and she will no longer produce the desired *admiración*. We can see a demagogical element in Prometeo's dealings with the populace. In spite of the refrain of the song in praise of Prometeo and his creation, it is not really true *ciencia* which the inhabitants are receiving, but an idol. Likewise, in the second act, they receive the use of fire, whose inner nature they do not understand but which gives them light and heat. When later in Act I the real Minerva descends from Olympus to speak to her worshipper, she does not object at all to the cult which Prometeo is forming around her; she thanks him, "no sólo agradecida / por tu estudioso empleo, / mas por el ara en que arde tu deseo" (p. 12). The term *ara* refers to the temple under construction, but also to Prometeo's devotion of courtly love (and by extension to Epimeteo's ardent desire for the statue). In Act II, there is a similar scene in which, after the statue comes to life, Epimeteo calls the populace together to show them what has happened. Prometeo arrives with the rest and asks for an explanation, but is silenced by the crowd: "[Q]ue ahora no hay para nada / atención, que no sea asombro" (p. 32). All thinking about the causes of this phenomenon ceases in order to give way to a feeling of astonishment based on ignorance.

The final element which binds the theme of knowledge to that of erotic love is the marriage between Prometeo and Pandora, a relation which has multiple facets: that of an artisan to his artifact, that of an intellectual to knowledge, and that of a lover to his beloved. The union which serves as *dénouement* to the whole play highlights Prometeo's artistic skill, his intellect, his will, and his sensorial appetite. The equating of a woman with a desirable *pequeño cielo* is a double-edged comparison. On the one hand, her sensorial beauty conveys the harmony and the untouchableness of immaterial objects.[8] On the other hand, the comparison introduces an element of self-interest and appetite which enters into conflict with Thomistic intellectualism.

Fire, light, and sun comprise another cluster of symbols whose content exceeds the conventional bounds set to the interpretation of the myth. The latter are given in Pérez de Moya's *Philosophia secreta,* which Valbuena Briones calls Calderón's immediate source and which he follows in his own interpretation of *La estatua.* First, notice that Prometeo, addressing the sun as the source of all light and knowledge, calls it "corazón del cielo." In the science of Calderón's age the heart was regarded as the seat of the emotions and of the life function itself, so that the sun symbol in this play cannot be taken only as a representation of abstract intellect or *lux naturalis* but also as a source of feeling. As regards fire, it cannot be emphasized enough that it signifies both light and heat, just as it is used in Renaissance love poetry to portray an emotion which illuminates at the same time that it is willful and destructive. Thus the play's central image has two facets: intellectual and emotional. Knowledge is prompted by desire and vice-versa.

The key to understanding the dual aspects of fire is the concept of instrumentality. Prometeo is known throughout as "el que da ciencia," yet he does not supply pure abstract knowledge, but rather something that is immediately useful or harmful. He cites a common opinion that censures "al que adquiere en patria ajena, / y no lo logra en la suya . . ." (p. 6). The verb *lograr* implies that knowledge must be realized or brought to fruition in tangible results before its effect can be considered complete. Epimeteo exemplifies the same tendency, since his way of showing veneration for the statue is to offer to build a temple, a feat which calls upon various arts and sciences to construct its "dóricas columnas" and "bronceados chapiteles." It is to be built in the form of a "piramidal aguja," which Sor Juana uses in the *Primero sueño* to symbolize the heights of speculative intellect. What is needed for such an undertaking is applied knowledge, just as Prometeo needed the art of sculpture to make his statue. While these uses of knowledge are intended for purposes on which all can agree, thought can also be used as a weapon when human beings disagree. When the rift occurs between Prometeo and Epimeteo, and the populace divides into two factions, Epimeteo declares all dialogue to be at an end and invokes the commencement of the battle with these words: "Ya no es tiempo, / si han de razonar las armas, / que lidien los argumentos" (p. 58). This sentence signifies first that weapons constitute the final source of right, as suggested by the inscription on several antique cannons: *Ultima Ratio Regum* ("the final reason of kings"); it also means that thoughts and arguments are weapons to be used when vital interests are at stake. In this case, the urgent question is: Shall mankind have the use of fire to improve the quality of life?

The Thomistic notion of contemplation is by no means refuted or overruled in the play. It continues to be asserted in remarks such as that of Pandora when the twin brothers begin to fight: "No más, que no es bien que a duelo / pase de la voluntad / la luz del entendimiento" (p. 40). One way of describing the philosophical climate of the play is to say that the dual Thomistic division of life into contemplation and activity is anything but clear in the figures of Prometeo and Epimeteo. Therefore the relation of reason to passions is modified, so that they become mutually dependent contraries, as symbolized in the identical horoscopes of the twins.

Another example of the way in which two opposing natures complement and mirror one another can be found in *En la vida todo es verdad y todo mentira*. The natural reaction of a Thomistic critic of this play would be to state that it reinforces the medieval idea of a world of false appearances which hides a core of truth and that since all is falsehood in this world, one must use "right reason" to solve its riddles. D. W. Cruickshank attributes this mode of thought to the hero Eraclio: "Eraclio . . . solves the difficulties by recognising that this life is a labyrinth, a dream, and that the real criteria are to be found elsewhere."[9] Such an interpretation, along the lines of A. A. Parker's criticism, does not seem to do justice to the play, since it is precisely the false appearance which becomes true at a later moment. It abstracts from the play a Machiavellian view of politics and life and a Thomistic one; then it assumes that Calderón endorses the latter. "The Thomistic view and the Machiavellian one are at odds. Now Calderón is a Thomist."[10] Eraclio and Leonido are seen as incarnations of these two views, and it is shown how it is logically and morally inevitable that Eraclio should be victorious at the end. This *a priori* method can be applied and has been applied successfully to many Calderonian *comedias,* but it robs the plays of a great deal of their variety and ultimately of the kernel that distinguishes Calderonian dramaturgy from a mere dramatized Thomism.

The general problem of this play is one of finding out a secret, and thereby it places itself squarely within the field of inquiry of this study of knowledge and emotions. The tyrant Focas must find out which of two young men, both raised as foundlings in the forest, is his own son and which the son of his archenemy Mauricio, the former emperor of Constantinople. The latter had been killed in battle when the bandit-conqueror Focas rose up against the Byzantine empire.

Focas has basically four sources which may provide the desired information; the first is Astolfo, the old man who raised the two boys and who has in his possession the medallion given to him by Focas' mistress when she died after giving birth to an illegitimate son. He withholds the secret because of his affection toward the young men, knowing that the one who is found to be Mauricio's son will be killed on the spot; therefore he refuses to speak even upon pain of death. Here at the outset we have a problem of knowledge inevitably linked to someone's vital interest. Astolfo's silence frustrates Focas in what he thought would be an easy method of obtaining information.

The second source is Lisipo, a magician who promises Focas that even before setting eyes on the young men, he will be able to divine which is which; he, however, is warned by Cintia, daughter of the former king of Trinacria (Focas' homeland), not to reveal anything; her motive is a natural sympathy she felt for the young men when she encountered them accidentally during a hunt in the forest. After this warning, Lisipo must feign an oracular frenzy in Focas' presence and exclaim that an "invisible goddess" (really Cintia, of course) has commanded him to remain silent. Thus another potential source of information is closed to the tyrant, who in spite of his military courage has a superstitious fear of omens and miracles.

Lisipo, despite the prohibition, is interested in gaining favor with Focas and sees no reason why he should not try to further his own interests as much as possible: "Y pues no estoy obligado / más que a guardar el secreto, / y le guardo—¿por qué no / trataré de mis aumentos?"[11] He makes a proposal to Focas which is enthusiastically received: he claims that by his magical science he can fabricate out of thin air a fantastic palace in which the events of one year in the lives of the two young men will be condensed into one day. Focas, Lisipo, and the two young men will be their real selves in this experiment, but Cintia, Libia, and the Calabrian ambassador of Duke Federico will be played by phantasms at the magician's command. Focas accepts because he hopes thereby to test the metal of the youths' personalities; one day will reveal to him everything he needs to know about them in order to make a correct judgement. As Cruickshank points out, he assumes wrongly that the young man whose behavior he most admires must be his own son and that whichever one shows hostility toward him must be Mauricio's son. Cruickshank attributes this assumption to a flaw, an unreasoned passionate nature, or an immorality in Focas.[12] I am not sure that this is a necessary premise for the play to make sense, but he is right in pointing out that Focas bases his experiment on an incorrect presupposition and that the tyrant does not carry his reasoning far enough.

Within the magic palace scenes, which cover the second part of Act II and the beginning of Act III and constitute the third source of information,

Focas, aided by Lisipo, devises four situations to test Eraclio and Leonido. The first test occurs when the two are brought to the palace and, after exchanging their savage animal fur clothing for courtly dress, are brought into Focas' presence. Eraclio, at this juncture, acts very humble, bows before the tyrant, kisses his feet, and makes a very flattering speech. We discover, however, from a short aside in the middle of this speech ("Tiranía, ¿qué no arrastras?"), that his humility is feigned and grudgingly enacted. Leonido, on the other hand, does not hide his contempt for Focas. When the latter asks him why he does not come forward to kiss his (Focas') feet like Eraclio, Leonido answers that he has no cause to be grateful, since he is of royal blood either from Mauricio or from Focas, and thus the life he leads while not yet in possession of royal power is odious to him, and Focas does him no favor in sparing his life. Focas is pleased both by the *rendimiento* of Eraclio and the *arrogancia* of Leonido; Eraclio's humility flatters the ruler's vanity while Leonido's prideful behavior mirrors his own arrogance and will to power. The first moment of testing provides no conclusive evidence.

Immediately afterwards (in the time of the play, but quite a bit later in the time of the condensed year), an ambassador of Calabria arrives with an arrogant diplomatic message from his lord: he requests that the latter be granted the Byzantine throne, since he is the closest male relative to the late Mauricio. Focas, of course, responds that the request is too presumptuous to be worthy of a response and closes the issue. Each of the two young men has his characteristic reaction to the message. Leonido, wanting to go further than Focas, is ready to throw the ambassador out of the palace window (this is an echo of Segismundo's reaction to one of his father's courtiers in *La vida es sueño*). Eraclio, believing in respecting the safeconduct granted to ambassadors, reminds his foster brother that although the message may be offensive, its words are not to be punished in the person of the ambassador. His distinction is almost Thomistic in its concern for the *ser propio* of a person as opposed to the function he carries out in society (or his *accidental* qualities). Once again Focas and Lisipo have a hard time deciding which reply pleases them more, so the doubt remains unresolved.

The third moment of testing involves the release of Astolfo from prison. Focas and Lisipo hide in the wings while the old man is restored to his adoptive sons. As would be expected, the sons differ in their reaction to this reunion: Leonido, with his usual arrogance, reproaches Astolfo, now that he knows himself to be the son of one ruler or another, for the many years during which the old man kept the boy in ignorance of the fact and for the uncivilized upbringing Astolfo has given him in the forest, when the old man must have known that he was bringing up a royal child. Eraclio, on the other hand, remembers the many good deeds Astolfo has done for them, especially the saving of their lives after their birth and the skills of hunting and natural lore which he has taught them. Focas is still equally pleased and equally confused by these new revelations of character, yet part of the irony of the play is that in the last act the same sequence is repeated with the roles reversed. Under changed circumstances, Eraclio reproaches the old man and Leonido defends him.

The final moment of testing comes when Focas pretends to fall asleep on a garden bench and has the phantasms of Cintia and Libia lead the young men into the garden and whisper in each one's ear that he is the son of Mauricio. The plan is to see which of the two, upon receipt of this news, will take advantage of the opportunity to wreak vengeance on Focas. Each one, after accepting the news as true without questioning, reveals his psychological reaction to the news in an aside. Leonido summarizes his thoughts thus: "Y pues en mí no ay más ley, / ni más raçón ni mas juycio / que desear reynar, qué hiciera / para poder conseguirlo?" (p. 127). In other words, Leonido realizes that the affection which he felt for Focas was due merely to his joy at being the son of a ruler, but now that he believes he knows exactly who his father was, he will do all he can to come into his own as soon as possible. Eraclio reacts to the news in a more internal and, in Thomistic terminology, a more *nonmaterial,* way: "Y pues no ay más ambición / en mí, ni deseo más digno / que el de ser quien soy, dejemos / lo demás de mis designios / al cielo, que él bolverá / por su causa" (p. 127). The repetition of the phrase *ser quien soy* is placed in quite a different context than in the honor plays; here it refers to the most interior essence of one's being. Eraclio does not try to exteriorize this knowledge; that is, he does not try to realize in the world the consequences of the power he knows to be his by right. He is content with the private knowledge that he is of royal blood.

In this scene, as in so many others in the play, Focas' plan backfires: the *mentira* which he had fabricated with Lisipo's help becomes a *verdad.* Until this point in the scene, he had only pretended to sleep, but was straining his ears to overhear the young men's soliloquies. Ironically, a heavy sleep overtakes him and the *sueño fingido* becomes a *sueño verdadero,* so that as the young men resolve in their own minds to act (or not to act in Eraclio's case), Focas is oblivious to everything that happens. Thus Leonido gets to the point of actually drawing his dagger before the tyrant awakes. When Eraclio leaves the stage for a few moments, Leonido seizes the opportunity to act, coming forward to the garden bench but not noticing that Eraclio has returned and has also advanced with his dagger drawn to protect Focas' life. As they both advance, Leonido shouts "¡Muera!" and Eraclio shouts "¡No muera!" The voices wake Focas, who in his twilight dream state had heard the two shouts but does not know which voice had pronounced which words; all he sees upon awakening is both young men with daggers drawn. Leonido tries to cover up his act with a lie, claiming that Eraclio had tried to commit murder and that he had drawn his weapon to protect the tyrant. Eraclio makes the same claim, but truthfully, of course.

Focas reacts immediately in a manner which uncovers a new psychological element in the play, an element which is his fourth source of information. In response to Eraclio's truthful self-defense, he shouts: "¡Mientes, mientes! Porque ya / que yo no pueda haçer juycio / de la voz ni de la acción, / por el pabor que (adiuino / el coraçón) desde el pecho / me dice en callados gritos, / tú eres el traydor, sí, ¡tú!" (p. 129). We are dealing with an almost instinctual reaction, which reveals one possible meaning of the play's title. In one sense, Focas' motive for turning against Eraclio is false, since it was Leonido who had tried to kill him. On another level, though, in turning against Eraclio, Focas is reacting in a natural fashion, since Eraclio is not his son but rather Mauricio's. The key to the irony lies in the fact that Focas, as Cruickshank points out, is a man of force and violence, and it is only logical that his son Leonido should resort to violence to obtain a throne, as Focas had done in his youth. "La fuerza de la sangre" makes Focas' true son turn against his father. Eraclio, on the other hand, is the son of Mauricio, a ruler who gained his throne by succession and not by force. So Eraclio's action shows the influence of his heredity when he leaves the determination of his fate to Providence.

The possibility of finding truth in a purely instinctive reaction is repeated in the last scenes of the play, after Eraclio and Astolfo have been banished by Focas and set afloat in a leaky boat without a rudder. They are rescued by Duke Federico, Mauricio's nephew. The recognition scene between the two blood relatives of the former emperor is again one of instinct, since Federico says: "[P]ues la sangre de mi pecho / (tan tuya como ser hijo / de Casandra, hermana vella / de Mauricio) nuestra estrella / confronta" (p. 155). Here the heart, seat of emotions and of the blood, gets at the truth more directly than reason.

All of Focas' methods fail excepting the last, which seemed least likely to succeed. In terms of the play's title, it is a *mentira* which supplies the *verdad*; it is Focas' instinctive fear of Eraclio (what Thomistic psychology would define as *fuga,* a nonrational avoidance of something perceived as harmful) which turns out to be the revealing factor. In fact, when Astolfo and Lisipo, who have always known the secret, reappear onstage after the magic palace sequence, they are amazed to find that Focas has "guessed" the truth by what is called in present-day Spanish a *corazonada.*

There is an irreducible positive element of instinct and emotion in this play which refuses to fit into the Thomistic scheme. It consists of a passion (in the old sense of something undergone) which triggers a mental process which had been frustrated until that moment of the action. Cruickshank, by not recognizing this factor, ends up with a rather uninteresting protagonist and admits as much: "Eraclio is, alas, somewhat dull as a result. Most virtuous characters are."[13] Eraclio need not be seen as dull if it is not presupposed that he represents "virtue" and that poetic justice guarantees him his just deserts from the very beginning.[14]

Most of Cruickshank's observations are made from the point of view of the *dénouement*. Perhaps it would be wiser to take into consideration the successive moments of the drama in their own right, each with its partial stage of knowledge, leaving open-ended elements even in the last scene. In other words, as we have hinted earlier, the drama is not seen as an action over a certain lapse of time during which certain processes occur. It is true that at the end of the play one side wins out, but until that moment Leonido's point of view is represented with as much intensity and persuasiveness as Eraclio's. If we can say that the Stoic-Thomistic point of view is the "correct" one in an abstract sense, we can also say that the advocates of will to power, pragmatism, and ambition put up an impressive fight and there are moments in which the latter view has its truth. Also, there are many incidents in which Eraclio performs an action that Leonido will repeat later on, but with a different motivation. The play's title backs this up when it declares that *"all* is true and *all* is false." Any speech or action may have several aspects, depending on the circumstances of its execution. We cannot distinguish an absolute truth or an absolute ethic in this *comedia* unless we, in the manner of Parker, look "elsewhere" for a standard. In the light of such a standard, sense can be made of the play, but it yields an interpretation which is less rich and profound than the material Calderón has offered his audience. The title of the early published editions reads *En esta vida* . . . , a wording which lends itself to the possibility of judging the actions in terms of another life such as we find portrayed in the *autos sacramentales*. The manuscript which Cruickshank uses, however, reads *En la vida* . . . , thereby encouraging us to concentrate on the causes and effects of the characters' lives as empirically tested and observed in the situations into which they are thrown by Focas and by the playwright-experimenter Calderón.

Thus the problem of obtaining knowledge is represented in this *comedia* by a sort of "play-within-a-play" structure. The magic palace scenes constitute a separate theatrical performance which resembles a scientific experiment in that there are both controlled objects (the phantasms of Cintia and Libia, the garden bench set-up, etc.) and objects which are being tested (the characters of the two princes). Magical artifice is being used to obtain knowledge, just as in Renaissance science, data was being collected about natural phenomena. Focas' and Lisipo's observations bring concrete results, but unfortunately the experimenters are unable to interpret their data. Since all is truth and all is falsehood, various conclusions can be drawn from the experienced phenomena and thus no definite answer can be had by this method. The tyrant and the magician, however, who are performing this experiment are subject to the manipulation of Calderón, who exercises complete control over his dramatic world. The latter's purpose is really the opposite of that of Focas, since he starts with an abstract principle expressed in the play's title and sets about corroborating the principle with a particular example. He is not trying to obtain new knowledge.[15] So *En la vida* offers us a peculiar combination of medieval deductive procedure and Renaissance induction. Underlying both of these ways of thinking are the passions; that is, the vital interests that are at work before rational experimentation begins. Within the play, we are confronted by Lisipo's desire to win Focas' favor as well as Focas' desire to find his own son and kill his archenemy's son. Outside the play we find a whole set of emotional responses in the aristocrats and intellectuals of seventeenth-century Spain, whose keynote Calderón was able to strike so accurately in each of his *comedias*. I am referring to a strange mixture of imperial willfulness, Stoic resignation, asceticism, and love of wit and artifice as well as other tendencies which combine to produce expressions like *En la vida todo es verdad y todo mentira*. It was not abstract intellectual speculation that led Calderón and his contemporaries to choose titles like *Darlo todo y no dar nada, Primero es la honra que el gusto*, and *Más vale maña que fuerza*. These titles, being preestablished before Act I begins, put a burden on the dramatic action, thus requiring providential intervention, i.e., Calderón's heavy-handed but playful coincidences. The ideological pressure on the *dénouement* becomes even stronger, and the operation of coincidence (disguised as God's providence) even more necessary as we move on to the *comedias de santos*.

5

Comedias de santos

If we return to our premise that Calderonian dramas depend for their representations on sensorially accessible elements, we will discover some key concepts that are indispensable in attacking the knotty problems posed by the religious dramas, from which we will select *Las cadenas del demonio* and *El mágico prodigioso* for close examination. A full-scale Calderonian stage production involves words spoken by characters whose bodies move onstage, certain *apariencias* (supernatural apparitions), *tramoyas* (angels and gods descending *ex machina*), and finally a stage setting (which becomes increasingly elaborate in the later plays which Calderón wrote for the Buen Retiro and the Palacio de la Zarzuela). The verbal and visual limits of such a medium become extremely problematic when the dramatic subject matter includes invisible and intangible, that is, spiritual, beings. The Thomistic principle with which I began this study, namely, that nonmateriality places a being in an intrinsically higher realm of the hierarchy of the universe, comes up against a form of expression, the theater, which seems least likely to be able to put across such a principle adequately. In short, the problem which presents so many obstacles to an understanding of the *comedia de santos* is a combination of the dramatic treatment of God's intervention in human affairs, the Devil's temptation of human beings, and the workings of free will in human salvation.

In the case of divine intervention, we are faced with the following problem: God is a nonmaterial and invisible being and, as the Old Testament claims, no man has seen his face. Therefore he cannot appear *per se* on the Calderonian stage. Yet in Calderón's *comedias* God's influence is often of paramount importance to the action. Orthodox theology states that the invisible God's will and revelation are made known to man from time to time through his messengers, the angels, who are themselves nonmaterial beings that can take on visible forms. This is one way in which Judaeo-Christian theology has tried to bridge the gap between an invisible, eternal God and a material, temporal human race. In Calderón's secular theater, the problem appears to be not so much a literary one as one of stagecraft, since in many cases Calderón has a figure dressed as an angel descend *ex machina* to deliver a message to the human characters. In other situations, he employs offstage "disembodied" voices that sing God's message, but in either case the theatricality of the devices is transparent.

Another problematic aspect of these supernatural phenomena is that they interrupt the dramatic chain of cause and effect which constitutes the rules of the game in secular drama. The idea of dramatic craftsmanship (which neither Lope nor Calderón always exercised to the full) demands a well-knit play in which there are no arbitrary elements. Yet Calderón's *comedias* are full of coincidences, especially such plays as *La dama duende,* in which characters enter and leave the stage mysteriously, letters arrive and disappear by themselves, and two characters just happen to meet in a dark room at a strategic moment. Behind all these dramatic surprises, the reader can see Calderón, the creator and sole manipulator of his drama, inventing a series of coincidences to provoke certain emotions. Just as in *La dama duende* Calderón wants to provoke humorous amazement in his spectators, so in the supernatural plays he wants to create a devout mystery which nevertheless shows its own artificiality by its *ex machina* placement within the plot. The devices have little to do with the human motivations involved, but rather cut directly across the dramatic fabric. In the *comedias de santos,* apparitions of angels and stage miracles attempt to further the stage action by introducing divine causation, but this very attempt ends up interrupting the chain of *human* causes and effects that constitutes a drama in its original Greek meaning of "action," "something enacted."

The only logic one could use to make this arbitrary intervention fit into the whole of the play is a logic and a method of criticism which is itself Augustinian or Thomistic, and which posits the inner invisible workings of grace and free will as the "real" drama of which the human circumstances are the outside shell.[1] The *comedias de santos* then become more *autos* than *comedias,* since their inner kernel is not a human situation, but a divine one; what goes on in the invisible realms of heaven and hell and what transpires imperceptibly in the characters' free will is more important than the sensorially perceptible events that are presented to the audience. In this way, an angelic appearance or a celestial voice, whether perceived collectively or individually, comes as no surprise. In fact, it becomes the crux of the spiritual "dramatic" action.

We must go back to the Thomistic concepts of activity and passivity in order to understand Calderón's elaboration of supernatural events. It is not necessary here to go into detail on the exact theological arguments of the period, since our purpose is to characterize not Calderón's "doctrines," but the dramatic presentation of them. In our first chapter, we discussed St. Thomas' (and in general Suárez') doctrine that the intellect, being the most active and the least material of mankind's faculties, is the best suited to guide human beings along the right path of life; this is really Aristotelian doctrine and does not originate with Scholasticism. For a Christian, however, the active intellect also has a passive side in that the power of reasoning is a gift of God and that the *lux naturalis* which enables us to abstract intelligible species from matter comes from God. Without him none of our faculties could perform its function, so just where human beings may consider themselves most active, and free from outside force, theology is compelled to say that this activity is the result of grace. Catholicism adds that free, active reason should follow the dictates of the Scriptures, the Fathers, and the Church, since it is only reasonable that the words which proceed from God be accepted as truth. St. Thomas attempts to reconcile the omnipotence of God as *prima causa* of all things with the metaphysical Aristotelian doctrine of intellect (*noûs*) as the authentic determinant of man's highest actions. Yet his doctrine on the subject contains a tension which eventually resulted in the Báñez-Molina disputes and the Jansenist controversy. (These disputes were generally over *will* and grace, yet one of the will's technical names in Scholastic theology is *appetitus intellectivus.*)

In large portions of Calderón's *comedias,* this problem does not come out directly; in the matrimonial, political, and philosophical plays, God's intervention does not constitute an organic part of the plot (with the exception of *Los cabellos*). It is possible to see the codes of ethics which the characters do *not* follow and which bring about their downfall as divinely ordained, but this adds nothing positive to the play's content. Again, it is possible to postulate a divine intervention or inner spiritual change which would have taken place if the characters were not pagans or had not allowed themselves to be overwhelmed by passions, but this also tells us nothing about the actual events of the play.[2] Feuerbach once observed that to deny miracles is to deny God, for if the possibility of Nature's laws being broken is inconceivable, then there is no reason to postulate a special Providence; likewise, if no celestial voices can intrude on a person's thought processes, then it is indifferent and senseless to say that every virtuous thought comes from God and every evil thought from the Devil. Therefore, it seems logical to speak of the workings of grace only in those plays which contain miracles, the *comedias de santos,* in which certain wondrous events are attributed undeniably to God and not to magic, Nature, or chance.

In this study on dramatic psychology, the "miracle" that we must deal with is that of conversion, an occurrence which represents the same interruption of cause and effect in the human psyche as external miracles do in the laws of Nature. There are three case studies of conversion in the plays under consideration: Irene and Licanoro in *Las cadenas del demonio* and Cipriano in *El mágico prodigioso.*

The title of *Las cadenas del demonio* gives an indication of the play's characteristics: it can be thought of as a theologico-military drama, since the battle of the Gospel against the Devil and his pagan idols depends largely on miraculous physical force and very little on theological arguments. The only extended debate between San Bartolomé and the Devil resembles a duel more than anything else, and it ends with the Devil prostrated at the saint's feet, just as in countless Calderonian battle scenes. The chains mentioned in the title remind the reader of the victims in a triumphal procession, thus completing the process of turning an eternal spiritual conflict into an almost earthly war.

There are two types of chains present in the drama and both are manifested physically at some point: the chains which Satan uses to subject human beings to his will, which appear in the form of bodily demonic possession, and the chains which San Bartolomé is authorized by God to place upon the Devil; these become actual chains of fire which keep Satan fastened in a cave until one of his human accomplices releases him. Ultimately, the play's outcome depends upon which side can wield more powerful "magic" (in the Devil's case) or "miracles" (in the case of San Bartolomé).[3] We cannot distinguish between the two supernatural adversaries according to the beneficent or harmful effects of their works, since the Devil performs various "good" works, such as freeing Irene from her prison.

Irene, daughter of the King of Lower Armenia, is a female counterpart of Segismundo, in that from her birth she has been kept locked in a tower by her father because of an unfavorable prophecy made about her. In her opening monologue, she threatens to commit suicide out of despair and offers her body and soul to any power that can free her. The Devil accepts her offer and promises to free her, a promise which he keeps. Since he appears to her in the form of a young man, we can assume that Irene, who has never seen a man before, is also being tempted sexually. The Devil in this initial stage represents to her everything of which she has been deprived, freedom, power, and love, since the Devil magically allows her to see her handsome young cousins Ceusis and Licanoro through the walls of her father's palace. From this point on, Irene's enslavement to the Devil goes through three stages which correspond to the three acts of the play, until she is released in Act III by San Bartolomé.

The Devil obtains Irene's release from the tower by speaking through the idol of the local god Astarot to the king, who, as a devout worshipper of his gods, complies with this command. Irene comes to the temple to give thanks for her release at the very moment that San Bartolomé approaches proclaiming Christ as the true Savior. Irene is one of the first to demand that the saint be put to death. At this stage her enslavement is limited to a sense of duty to the god who gave the command that she be freed, "pues como esclava / me toca del dios Astarot la ofensa."

Irene's first entrance in Act II shows her melancholic and seeking diversion in music, exactly like Mariene in *El mayor monstruo* shortly before her death and Fénix at the beginning of *El príncipe constante,* both of whom are women who consider themselves oppressed by fate. Irene is conscious of her own enslavement and is made melancholic by a new, contradictory feeling that has entered her heart: she has fallen in love with Licanoro, but cannot be united with him since he is in favor of the new religion which San Bartolomé is preaching. He is also attracted to her, but refuses her request that the saint be put to death. All through Act II Irene is in this problematic position, until the end of the act when her actual demonic possession is foreshadowed. San Bartolomé and the Devil (the latter disguised as a prophetess) engage in a medieval theological debate, and after the Devil's defeat, San Bartolomé orders him to abandon forever the idol of Astarot. The Devil must comply, but warns the saint that he is planning to reside in a better, living statue, referring of course to Irene.

In Act III Irene's exclamation upon accepting the demonic pact ("¡Ay! rabiando vivo, ¡ay! rabiando muero") becomes literally true. She has a characteristic mad scene in which she speaks with the Devil's voice and arouses terror and pity in her fellow courtiers. Yet her words to her father, to San Bartolomé, and to her two suitors have elements of truth, causing the king to pronounce a very Calderonian paradox: "Que estás loca, ahora / creo que con más ocasión, / porque dicen que verdades / dicen los locos."[4] The Devil is thus speaking the truth, albeit a sarcastic one, through his instrument. Irene has not lost the power of feeling jealousy over Licanoro's rejection of her, which means that she has not lost her capacity to love; Licanoro describes the situation in a manner which is extremely puzzling from a Thomistic point of view: "¡Qué haya razón para celos / aún adonde no hay razón!" (I, 668). This second paradox stretches to its highest tension the Scholastic problem of passions: To what extent is Irene deprived of reason and occupied by another power? To what extent do her evil thoughts originate in her own mind? In other words, is her temptation an internal or external event? Many traditional analyses make the Devil's influence in the *comedia* a symbol for a process which goes on in the mind and which the subject consents to. Yet here we have an example in which a woman's own speech and mental discourse are blocked out by another mind and voice, an extreme example of the classical definition of passion. On the other hand, when San Bartolomé begins to practice the exorcism on Irene, is this not also an example of a passion, of something which is done to her rather than of her own doing? For one dramatic moment, San Bartolomé and the Devil engage in a sort of spiritual tug-of-war over Irene's body and soul. How can this be thought of as a conversion in the manner of, let us say, St. Augustine?

Calderón's solution to the problem was satisfactory for his time, but for the modern reader it creates more problems than it solves. He combines force and free will in the same scene. San Bartolomé uses force to drive the Devil into one little hair on Irene's head, since the Devil was controlling her body by force. Once her speech and intellect are temporarily free, Irene uses her free will to repent of having sold herself to the Devil. If the saint had not used supernatural influence to free her, she would have remained possessed, so her conversion is only partially a result of her own decision. Theologically, that is, conceptually, this contradiction can be and has been resolved. Volumes were written on the subject in Counter-Reformation Spain. Faced with the externality of the stage, however, the problem of conversion has to resort to arbitrary theatrical devices and outward stage machinery to insure that both grace and free will play their part in this conversion.[5]

The case of Licanoro presents the opposite problem: he displays the required inwardness, the doubts and speculations of an Augustine, but he does not really undergo a conversion in the sense of an identifiable turning point. He is already half a Christian when he makes his first entrance. In Act I he enters discussing a passage from the book of Genesis with the priest of Astarot. He is obsessed with the idea that there is one true God, very much as the secular Prometeo is obsessed with the idea of divine wisdom in Minerva. None of the pagan priest's arguments can sway him from his search for this one "unknown god." As soon as San Bartolomé arrives at the temple and preaches Christ as the one God he is looking for, Licanoro becomes fascinated with the new doctrine. He does not persecute the saint as the king, Irene, and Ceusis do. Yet this same scene in the temple contains the moment at which he falls in love with Irene. The division of his loyalties is made visible in the way in which Irene's first entrance is immediately followed by that of San Bartolomé. The sight of a beautiful woman is followed by the sight of a haggard, ugly "living skeleton" with sackcloth and ashes. What he seeks from this obscure man is light concerning the identity of the God that the latter is preaching.

In Act II, the division of loyalties becomes sharper, since the beautiful woman asks Licanoro to kill the saint. But Licanoro, like Eraclio in *En la vida,* chooses a long-term happiness over an immediate gratification, although this represents no change in his character, since from the beginning he has been contemplative, moderate, and tolerant. The disposition of his will, his *natural,* is that of a Christian. All he needs is the intellectual confirmation that the sole God he seeks is the same as San Bartolomé's Christ. It is not possible to point out a moment of conversion in which his will is changed, unless it be the moment when San Bartolomé defeats the Devil in Scholastic disputation and all present exclaim "¡Viva Cristo!" or the moment when Irene is freed from the Devil's power and accepts Christianity, so that Licanoro's love for her is no longer in contradiction with his belief in San Bartolomé's doctrine. Calderón, by killing two dramatic birds with one stone, has deprived Licanoro of the chance to develop as a character by the overcoming of dilemmas, as happens with the husbands of honor and Decio. His obstacle to happiness is miraculously removed and, in gratitude to the new God, he offers to build a temple.

In a very uncharacteristic fashion, Calderón revives the seeds of conflict in Licanoro after the spiritual battle is apparently won. Licanoro and Irene are married, and in one of the last scenes of the play, Irene is in their bedroom, waiting for Licanoro to return. The Devil, having been freed from his chains of fire by the envious brother Ceusis, returns for one last attempt to gain Irene's soul. She resists his temptation with her new-found faith, but while they are conversing Licanoro returns, hears voices, and hides in the wings to overhear. Just when this newlywed couple's salvation seems assured, Calderón throws us back to jealousy, the most deep-seated passion in his dramatic repertoire. We have seen how jealousy can upset political regimes; now we see how it endangers salvation. Licanoro, thinking that Irene has had a tryst with a human lover, will not listen to her protestations, but rather prepares to kill her like a true Calderonian nobleman. The only escape is a miraculous one: celestial voices that remind him that he is now a Christian, whereupon he lays down his sword. This abrupt injection of a deadly passion after conversion is an anomaly in Calderón's works, but it is one indication among many of the fact that the ethic of these plays is unavoidably aristocratic. Calderón's *soy quien soy* must include matrimonial honor as long as the character is of noble blood. In the world of the *comedias,* conversion to Christianity does not involve relinquishing aristocratic status or behavior. San Bartolomé, in his role as apostle, may refuse the royal purple and the laurel wreath offered by the King of Armenia, but the king himself, Irene, and Licanoro remain rulers, although their state religion is now Christianity. Whether the aristocratic or the Christian side of ethics is uppermost in Calderón's works is a highly debatable question, but it is certain that neither aspect drops out of the picture, even in his most religious *comedias.*

In contrast to the rather obvious construction of *Las cadenas,* with its dependence on external devices, *El mágico prodigioso* presents not only a better constructed play but also a greater reliance on inner thought processes as elements of conversion. One of the two protagonists, Justina, is already a Christian, and her dramatic struggle consists in resisting temptation. Cipriano, on the other hand, begins as a pagan and ends as a Christian. He resembles Licanoro in that he begins the play with a theological doubt. However, Cipriano must go through a great deal of practical experience before reaching salvation, whereas Licanoro jumps directly from speculation to belief. Yet Cipriano's process of conversion, although it is one of the most artfully crafted in Calderón's works, still runs up against the problem of theatricality.

In the first place the Devil's intervention continues to be problematic. By presenting him as a more fully developed *human* character, Calderón runs three "risks": (1) investing the Devil with a certain grandeur, thus making him more sympathetic, (2) making him into a rival of God as a cosmic power in his own right, and (3) causing the human character and the Devil to confront each other as man to man, enabling the latter to exert a direct personal influence on the other's will.[6] All of these tendencies can be found in *El mágico* if the reader approaches it without first arming himself exclusively with Scholastic doctrine in order to insure that he will arrive at a "correct" interpretation of the play.

To show how the Devil is invested with positive qualities, it is only necessary to turn to the two scenes in which he introduces himself to Cipriano in two different disguises: first as a learned nobleman and later as a nobleman turned pirate. In the first case he shows his skill in Scholastic dialectic by answering all of Cipriano's questions, but is led into an intellectual blind alley and must admit that Cipriano's affirmation of one God is correct. He sustains a good polemic and only gives in because Cipriano comes up with the true doctrine of the unity and trinity of God, which the Devil cannot deny. The argument could have continued *ad infinitum*, but Calderón cuts it off by having Cipriano declare an infallible theological truth (although it is hard to see how this complex doctrine follows from Cipriano's previous arguments). He also has the Devil hear offstage voices approaching. The cutoff is rather arbitrary, both in terms of dogma and of theatrical techniques, but it is an arbitrariness which is perfectly consonant with Calderón's medieval aspect: the Devil is highly intelligent, but he *must* lose the argument against official Church dogma.

In his second appearance to Cipriano, the Devil has a twofold character: pirate and magician. As a defiant pirate who has dared to challenge the King of Kings, he shows the characteristics of a hero and applies to himself many of the same terms which were given a positive connotation in the characterization of Herodes, Decio, and Leonido; he calls himself "bizarro" and refers to his "alientos briosos" and his "lustre tan heroico."

As a magician, the Devil displays superhuman knowledge, especially practical knowledge which can be used to bring about certain physical effects. In this respect, Cipriano resembles Goethe's Faust in that for both of them, "In the beginning was the deed."[7] Cipriano befriends the Devil because the latter promises to acquire Justina for him. The Devil swears that he will be a loyal friend until death, which would have turned out to be a true promise if Cipriano had not repented.[8] He does not tell his victim, however, that he does not have the power to bring the real Justina into Cipriano's possession. So in regard to the theological "risk" of presenting the Devil as a cosmic rival of God, the answer is that in *El mágico* this is plainly the case. There is a visible wonder worker, Satan, who makes the *tramoya* of the mountain move at his verbal command, and an invisible wonder worker, God, whose works are represented by other *tramoyas* and *apariencias,* such as the figure of the skeleton under Justina's cloak and the storm and earthquake phenomena at the moment of Justina's and Cipriano's death. Theologically it may be objected that the Devil's power is only granted to him by God, who is the sole controller of the universe, but dramatically the Devil and God are pitted against each other as rivals, the Devil losing, of course, because orthodoxy and moral indignation require it.

The third "risk," that of allowing the Devil to exert a direct external influence on the will of his victims, also becomes unavoidable in the dramatic genre, since drama is, as we have said, a chain of causes and effects. Theology intends to safeguard free will by insisting that the Devil "cannot . . . act directly upon the human intellect; internally he can only act upon the imagination and the sensitive appetite. Externally he can act upon the senses."[9] Yet a drama generally has its effect in the traceable pattern of events in which one step leads to another by a process that the spectators of the play consider valid. If arbitrary events are introduced, they must be of a sort which the spectator is trained to accept (e.g., we accept as convention the ludicrous coincidences and the hiding in closets and under beds of a French bedroom farce). The spectator must be able to follow how a character gets from point A to point B or to overlook the arbitrary elements because of his conditioning as an audience member.[10] The conversion and successful resistance of temptation in *El mágico* partake of both of these factors. They are a way of explaining the final outcome and a way of avoiding an explanation of an outcome that is predetermined. Free will in Calderón is an instrument for carrying forward the plot (as when Justina resists the demonic voices) but it is also a way of bridging moments that are essentially arbitrary.[11]

Justina's temptation scene, for example, has a much better dramatic preparation than most scenes in *Las cadenas,* but it still contains certain hiatuses that reveal its doctrinal function, which is to present the triumph of free will in a simplified form of the doctrine. The basic constituent elements are a human subject with a rational soul, a passion which threatens to overwhelm the soul, and a free rational will which does not give in to the passion. In Act I, Calderón had prepared the passion by having Justina fall in love at first sight with Cipriano, although her resistance to this love never wavers in the first two acts. On seeing Cipriano for a second time, Justina confides in an aside that since she saw him she has had no peace, but she treats him with virtuous disdain all the same. Before her Act III entrance, the Devil announces that he will tempt her by presenting erotic images and sounds to her senses. Offstage voices begin to sing "Amor, amor" as Justina enters. She wonders about the pain she feels and the phantasms in her brain. The music responds that this is love. Then Justina begins to describe, in *culteranista* terms, the natural erotic phenomena around her: a nightingale singing to his mate, a vine clinging to a tree, and a sunflower turning toward the sun. The question arises: Are these natural events or images conjured up by the Devil? Justina calls them "deceptively appealing" and resists their appeal. Yet they represent the natural inevitability of love. Do they also belong to the Devil? There is a blending of natural sights and sounds with supernatural voices, all represented artificially on a theatrical stage. Moreover, the flower, vine, and bird images are only accessible to us through Justina's words. If we take the images as symbolic of thoughts in the heroine's mind, then the sense of temptation is lost, and instead of being, like Cipriano, part of a cosmic struggle,[12] Justina has a conflict within herself. In that case, we could say that her love-distraught mind interprets the natural sights and sounds as erotic suggestions.[13] The fact is that there are offstage voices reinforcing the message of love, so that we must admit at least some element of external temptation in this scene. The externality becomes more apparent when the Devil appears in person and tries to drag Justina to where Cipriano awaits her. He tugs at her but cannot budge her feet; the weak woman is stronger than the angel in human form. Finally she says the magic word, *Dios,* which immediately causes the Devil to release her and disappear. Calderón saves the utterance of this word until the end of the scene for dramatic effect and also to point out the theological idea that the free will is only immovable when it allies itself with God. Yet a series of important paradoxes arises in these few lines of the play: What is the power that keeps Justina's feet on the ground, her own will or God? Most likely a long series of theological answers could be dug out of the writings of Molina and Báñez, but the problem here is one of theatrical logic. In this scene, unlike the climactic scenes of *Las cadenas,* God is represented by a word and by an immovable woman, without *tramoyas* and *apariencias.* The only stage deception is that of making the actor who plays the Devil pretend to exert strength and still not be able to move Justina. From the standpoint of the major British criticism, this reliance on symbolism and interior spiritual motivation makes *El mágico* one of Calderón's best religious *comedias,* yet when compared with *Las cadenas,* its very "spirituality" works against it. It leaves so much leeway for the characters' subjective interpretation of their feelings and perceptions that it opens the way for a broader human autonomy. In other words, a heavier reliance on speech in these scenes opens a way to a purely immanentistic interpretation of their dramatic psychology. Except for the bodily tug-of-war with the Devil, one could claim that in this scene Justina triumphs by her own force of will, which she believes by faith to be a gift of God.

Cipriano's conversion scene is the best prepared and most convincing of all the scenes we have dealt with, since there is a real process involved in the protagonist's change. Almost all of the dialogue and actions follow logically, from the moment when Cipriano complains to the Devil that he has not fulfilled his part of the bargain until the moment when Cipriano transfers his allegiance to the Christian God. The logic that holds this part of the action together is Cipriano's self-interest in love and later in spiritual salvation. If we see this scene in almost mercantilist terms, we can understand its movement better than that of Justina or Irene, whose minds and bodies are tossed back and forth between God and the Devil.[14] It may be true that Cipriano has "blundered into a cosmic struggle," but in his participation in this struggle his aim is to save himself and to obtain his heart's wishes. What he discovers at the end of his bargaining is that no human or angelic dealer can give him what he wants. Yet he has made a seemingly unbreakable contract by selling himself as a slave to the Devil. His only aim after this realization is to get out of his contract, and he gives himself unconditionally to the only one who is more powerful than the Devil and who only bargains absolutely.

Both reason and will are at work in this scene: Cipriano had been given false information by the Devil, and he forces Satan by means of the latter's own magic to tell him about the God who protects Justina. As the Devil confesses the omnipotence and the supreme goodness of God, Cipriano immediately connects this information with his theoretical quandary about the definition of God at the beginning of the play. He resolves to transfer his allegiance, but the Devil reminds him of the contract. Since this contract was based on false information, however, Cipriano is free from its obligations if he repents of the crime of allying himself with God's enemy. Cipriano is in a position in which he has no other choice but to be rescued.

In consonance with Catholic orthodoxy, of course, this higher being is not only all-powerful but all-good, so that the hero's release from the Devil is also an escape to an eternal blessedness, but only after a martyr's death. His ready acceptance of martyrdom is one of the great hiatuses of the last act. His turning to God has been motivated by fear of what the Devil's contract implied, yet when he appears in a frenzied state before the Governor and the people (much like Irene before her exorcism), he is eager to bring glory to the God who has withheld Justina from him throughout the play and who is permitting him to die without possessing her. His reward for this deprivation is summarized by the Devil in the last scene: "[L]os dos, a mi pesar, / a las esferas subiendo del sacro solio de Dios, / viven en mejor imperio" (p. 229). This better life is only grasped by faith, not reason, so that the conclusion of the play constitutes another victory for faith.[15] Cipriano seems to the Governor and his son to have "lost his reason," and this is true to the extent that Cipriano has left off reasoning for particular ends and goods and has made a radical turn to an invisible *summum bonum,* namely, the one we described in our first chapter. Yet for secular reason, i.e., for the ultimately pragmatic thinking that in Calderón's *comedias* escapes temporarily from the hierarchical existence of the *autos,* both of the characters who surrender their will to a supernatural power (Irene to the Devil and Cipriano to God) appear as mad. Between these two stand the characters who form the heart of the non-Thomistic elements in Calderón: autonomous human beings involved in practical human activity.

In the three permanently pagan noblemen in the play, we can see how the honor code and reasons of state exist alongside the God-man relationship, forming dramatic situations and patterns that really belong to the matrimonial and political plays. Lelio and Floro are familiar *galanes* from Calderón's cloak and sword comedies; the fact that the Devil intervenes in these scenes in no way changes the Lopesque pattern of mistaken identity and chance encounters.

The Governor of Antioch behaves like any Calderonian prince, and the fact that he persecutes Christians does not make him any less of a "prudent" monarch in the handling of affairs of state.

As we have examined one by one the various systems of behavior that Calderón puts to dramatic use, we have seen that these systems do not cancel each other out, but that each has a relative autonomy that brings it into conflict with the others. Christian behavior is probably the least developed of these systems in the *comedias*; the actions and words of Irene and Cipriano after conversion are far less interesting than Don Gutierre's monologue on honor or Absalón's political machinations. In fact, saintliness more often than not depends on the other realms of being to provide it with metaphors: the *gracioso* Clarín calls Cipriano "el mágico de los cielos"; there is another *comedia* entitled *Los dos amantes del cielo*, and Lope de Vega has one called *El rústico del cielo*. Divine intervention is something added onto worldly systems that have their own logic and in which reason and the passions alternately hold sway. In the *comedias*, moral theology need not be the key to understanding honor, politics, and the problem of knowledge, unless we feel obliged to bring it in from the outside. It is possible to do just this, but one must be careful not to assume that this is Calderón's procedure. Where he brings in God and the supernatural, they do not perform the unifying function one might expect but rather become one more force fighting for the characters' loyalty. If divine force wins in Act III of these *comedias*, this happens through a playful tendency in Calderón's style that cannot leave the dramatic situation unredeemed but must find a way, even through stage devices, to end the play with an apotheosis. Dramatically this was, and perhaps still is, effective, but for the critic who is trying to reconstruct Calderón's world view, it helps very little in his effort to patch up the ideological cracks which separate one realm of human behavior from another.

6

Conclusion

The examples that we have chosen from Calderón's dramaturgy have progressively revealed an element which the majority of ethical critics of Calderón either have overlooked or have established as one of the factors in human life that Calderón "condemns": pragmatic instrumentality. The Thomism which so many critics attribute to Calderón (and very rightly so) deals with means, ends, and final causation, but always with an eye toward the *summum bonum,* the Catholic God, who, because he is immaterial, omnipresent, and omnipotent, cannot be an object of man's manipulation. In other words, medieval Thomism emphasizes the idea that man's grasping and utilization of his world must end at a point where man is himself grasped by a higher reality. Unless this grasping in faith takes place, all the operations of the worldly man are in vain. To a large extent, this is the world of Calderón's *autos,* whose ideology comes from theologians of the medieval era.[1] The whole action is enveloped in the providence of God, who appears at the end of the *auto* in the form of the Eucharist to set the worldly situation straight. The characters' actions are hemmed in by the cradle and the grave; what lies beyond these barriers is of supreme importance but is not under the character's control except through correct behavior here on earth. There is a hierarchical order which, from the believer's point of view, determines what should be done. An unmanipulable but rational and supernatural sphere of being dictates conduct. To encourage such conduct in the spectator or reader is the whole objective of Calderón's dramatic *sermones en verso.*

The world of the *comedias* is one in which an opposite pattern encroaches on the domain of prescriptive ethics. The aristocrat's conduct is dictated to a great extent by other factors, by outside circumstances of a political, economic, or astrological nature, by considerations of social prestige, and finally by his irrational passions.[2] Action for these characters is not only project but also a response to the stimuli set in motion by nature, fate, or foreign political powers. Reason's function, therefore, is changed from that of dictating motives for action to that of justifying an action that has already been performed or has already been triggered by the emotions.[3] As we have mentioned, *ingenio* takes precedence over *juicio.* The mind sets out to invent reasons rather than to discover them. Yet the ideal of guiding one's actions by "right reason" still persists in the minds of Calderón's aristocratic and religious characters, so that, after finding a *sutileza* to fit the occasion, the will must cover up its tracks and the intellect must convince itself that reason was the original motivation. The ultimate exaggeration of this mental process can be seen in the satirical portrait of the Jesuit father in Pascal's *Provinciales,* who boasts gleefully that he and his colleagues have found theological opinions which allow confessors to absolve such sins as killing in duels and many forms of theft.

Thus, at countless moments in Calderón's secular works, we see reason being used as an instrument in the pursuit of goals that are perfectly worldly and concrete, or in response to the pressure of forces that are anything but divine and beneficent. When this happens, the character involved may or may not be conscious of how he is employing reason. In some cases, the character may be aware of his rationalization, but may also feel the need to anchor the reasoning process on an unquestioned principle.[4] So a whole arsenal of proverbs, maxims, and quotes from authoritative books are brought forward to supply intellectual weapons in the conflict of interests that lies at the base of each *comedia.* Everyone (even the *gracioso* in his absurd way) is ready to quote a general precept to defend his point of view, but there are so many different and conflicting authorities that the reader can see that for every concrete case there is a maxim to justify it; the *aplicación* precedes the *concepto.* The instrumentality of thought becomes transparent to the modern reader, but to the characters such a discovery always constitutes an exception to the rule, a case of faulty reasoning, or in classical terminology, a sophism. The overall Thomistic mental structure does not allow Calderón's characters to perceive that, ultimately, all of their reasoning is instrumental to some goal, even if that goal be spiritual salvation. (Yet the Jesuits were wont to proclaim that they were involved in the "business" [*negotium*] of man's salvation!)

These kinds of mental processes which subordinate reason to practical ends are, in fact, similar to those of the aristocratic class of late Hapsburg Spain. European politics had been secularized, at least in practice, and in spite of all the efforts to re-sacralize it, the effects of the development of a *razón de estado* could not be undone.[5] The Spanish high aristocracy was under an increased political and economic pressure as the seventeenth century progressed, until in 1640 Portugal seceded and Catalonia rebelled against Philip IV. The ruling class's defensive attitude imposed on the one hand a social urgency that is apparent in the authoritarian measures taken by the Count-Duke of Olivares, who "replaced the Duke of Lerma's Pharaonic pessimism with imperialistic dynamism."[6] In politics and economics, as well as in literature, "what is to be done" was dictated by outside pressures and the entire state bureaucracy and its *letrados* had to be made subservient to immediate needs.

Yet, these very attempts proved increasingly ineffective because of an ideology that could not envisage the new, often radical solutions proposed by liberal *arbitristas* such as González de Cellorigo and Pedro de Valencia. These included reforms of ecclesiastical property holdings, of the anti-manual work ethic of honor, and of Spaniards' attitudes toward money, commerce, and agriculture. There is little evidence in Calderón's work of the influence of these forward-looking thinkers who influenced Góngora.[7]

In Calderón almost no reasonable projects for mankind are put forth, outside of service to God, to the state in its absolutist and imperial form, or to one's noble lineage. The other forces at work are generally seen as irrational: erotic love, personal ambition, economic necessity, and astral determinism. This is not to say that they always carry a negative sign, only that they are regarded as asystematic or *desordenados*. Yet they gain a provisional justification in the service of the above-mentioned ideals.

The incongruities that appear when those behavior patterns conflict are evidence of cracks in Calderón's ideological edifice, cracks which the author could not fill in with another, sturdier material.[8] Thus the purely pragmatic motivations of many of his characters must be explained with the terminology and mental constructs of Scholasticism. For example, when in one scene character A lies vanquished at the feet of character B and in a later scene, B lies at the feet of A, the concept of Fortune is invoked: a term which does not explain the transition from one dramatic moment to another, but rather makes the spectator stand awestruck before this rapid reversal of circumstances. The only recourse for the Scholastic mind is to attribute the change either to the providence of God (which is basically inscrutable) or to an "erroneous" or "sinful" action on the part of the vanquished character, because according to Thomism punishment is only executed where sin has been committed. An aura of mystery (accompanied by exclamations of "¡Qué asombro!" "¡Qué admiración!" etc.) is created around a set of circumstances that European thinkers in other countries were on the road to explaining in scientific, political, or psychological terms.

The wonder and awe which the characters express is not merely a passive reflection of the confusion which occupied the consciousness of the Spanish aristocracy, but is also a contributor to that confusion.[9] Calderonian dramaturgy forms part of an ideology which attempted to re-feudalize Spain as the aristocracy felt its bases begin to slip away. Counter-Reformation theology, for example, is qualitatively different from medieval Thomism, since it was reaffirmed in an age that had experienced other currents of thought and activity which contradicted official belief.[10] When the old doctrines were reinstated under changed circumstances, they often could not adjust to the shift that had taken place and tended to remake or gloss over certain matters of fact.[11] The "dramatic craftsmanship" which Calderón exercised on earlier plays of other authors to emphasize an ethical or theological point should be seen as related to a larger educational (or re-educational) effort on the part of the absolutist monarchy and the Church, an effort which supplied not only the doctrines with which to interpret particular cases, but also the cases themselves. In Calderón's age, not only is the world a theater, but the theater is a world, carefully constructed by poets and intellectuals supported by the court aristocracy; the spectator, on his side, is trained to take this artistic spectacle and verbal artifice as the testing ground for ethical hypotheses instead of turning his attention to real life surroundings. For example, it is misleading to say that Calderón "shows" us that even in the most dire circumstances free will can liberate men, since the very *casus* which illustrates this doctrine is itself a product of Calderón's art.

This study may have left two conflicting impressions with the reader, which must be reconciled at this point, to the extent that such a reconciliation is possible. On one side, Calderón can be shown to be a consummate dramatic craftsman who leaves no ends untied at the close of each *comedia*. He is also admired for being able to entangle and disentangle the most intricate plots in his *comedias de capa y espada* without losing a thread, a feat which can also be seen in some of the more serious dramas we have studied. On the other side, critics like Constandse and Maraniss point out (with good reason) uncertainty and contradiction in the values used as motive forces in the secular plays. It seems to me that these two phenomena are related to each other. Calderón's *comedias* support both interpretations.

The *dénouement* of most of these plays is completely satisfying only if the reader or spectator accepts certain premises about virtue, vice, Providence, and free will. If disloyal, anti-Catholic, or dishonorable behavior is seen as passionate vice, that is, as a surrender to evil or unreal external impressions and the appetites they arouse, then virtuous behavior will be seen as a product of a spontaneous inner decision or of divine force through the infusion of grace. There are explicable motives like ambition, love, fear, greed, and jealousy, and inexplicable motives like conversion, visions and voices from heaven, and free will.

Of course, this simple division into natural and supernatural realms cannot adequately explain the behavior of Calderón's characters. The passions also have their inexplicable or unmotivated moments, usually within a soliloquy where the character makes an emotional turnabout or, after a long inner debate, decides impulsively upon a course of action. Likewise, explicable natural causes may be placed at the service of Providence (cf. the title of Calderón's play *Fuego de Dios en el querer bien*). In short, every exegete of the *comedias,* when inquiring after the why and how of the dramatic development, finds moments at which he can trace a tightly knit fabric of motivations. What a character does or thinks can be shown to be the outcome of his previous acts and thoughts. But he also finds moments at which the only answer to his question is "just because." If the character in question chooses an acceptable course of action, this lack of determinate motives is ascribed to free will, which is not a cause like other causes. If a character has an inexplicable impulse toward unacceptable behavior, the criterion of free will is generally *not* applied, but rather the behavior is traced to a demonic suggestion or an inordinate appetite. It would have been too upsetting to the value systems of Calderón's milieu to find examples of free will in gratuitously evil acts. Some characters, especially the well-known *bandolero* figures found in the works of several writers, may make this claim, but it is countered by many statements to the contrary, both in the *comedias* and the *autos*. This dilemma is not Calderón's alone, as the theological literature of the age shows, but in dramatic form it becomes even more problematic. The printed texts of the *comedias* contain no stage directions or prefaces to direct interpretation on this point and the scenic productions of this genre do not allow for allegorical figures like those of the *autos*, who can preach a clear moral lesson during and after the action. Calderón cannot interpose his own voice to tell us why an event occurs or why a character acts in a certain way. The plays are a mixture of the comprehensible and the inscrutable. If the first element were to disappear, there would be no *historia* (history or story), that is, no believable plots, not even devotional plots. If the element of the inscrutable were to disappear, we would be in the world of the deterministic drama of unredeemed fate and passion.

No matter how much or how little theology and Thomistic psychology can explain in these plays, it is beyond doubt that Calderón the craftsman uses both explicable and arbitrary elements to the fullest. He is really the opposite of a naturalistic playwright like Ibsen, for example. It is said that the latter rejected a "redeemed" ending for his *Doll's House* because he felt it would violate the logic of the psychological and social motivations which were the only ones he permitted himself. Like many other modern playwrights, he believed he was letting the *dénouement* "work itself out." Whether this actually happened or not is another issue. Calderón, on the other hand, often has a *dénouement* imposed by his historical or legendary sources. In order to make things turn out right or to bring a character to a certain pass which is necessary for the plot to run smoothly, he has several means at his disposal.

He may use a more or less deterministic set of motive forces to manipulate the situation. When he does this consistently, he comes close to the kind of well-articulated psychological processes found in individual characters like Othello, King Lear, and Racine's Phèdre, Bérénice, and others, and in dramas such as *La Celestina* and Machiavelli's *La Mandragola*, where the author takes great pains to assure that every step of character development or action is fully justified by the ruling motivations that he sets out from the beginning. Even some of Calderón's wildest coincidences can be explained by such natural motives. For example, one of several scenes in *La dama duende* in which the phantom lady is almost caught alone in Don Manuel's room as he enters from outside is caused by an understandable error of the valet Cosme. Don Manuel gives Cosme some papers to pack for their business trip to the Escorial and Cosme, being naturally talkative, puts the papers aside for a moment to ask his master some questions. Halfway along the road to their destination, Cosme realizes that he has left the papers behind, and Don Manuel is forced to return. The phantom lady, knowing of Don Manuel's travel plans, enters his room confidently and is not prepared when the travelers return unexpectedly. The construction of the scene in Don Manuel's room constitutes a sort of *deus ex machina* interruption, but the interruption has been meticulously prepared in a previous scene.

An almost diametrically opposed type of dramatic turn of events can be seen in *El mayor monstruo* when the Tetrarch hurls his dagger at the emperor Otaviano's back and a portrait of Mariene hanging over the doorway falls at that moment, causing the dagger to pierce the portrait and save the emperor's life. The incident is crucial to the action; if the dagger were to hit and kill the emperor (and woe to the stage production where the portrait mechanism fails), the play would be over. Yet there is no way of explaining why the portrait falls at that particular moment. The two scenes we have just described have one important element in common: they both constitute highly necessary turning points in the action, whether they are explicable or not. They are tools in the hands of a craftsman who knows where he is going.

However, if we abstract the various possible motivations that Calderón uses, we will find great obstacles to organizing them into a coherent system of values, especially in the case of notions that touch on theology, such as free will and grace. Even if the orthodox theology of the *autos* is applied, we are still left with the contradictions inherent in the currents of thought which Calderón used to compose those *autos*. It has been my task to demonstrate this affirmation throughout the present study. So we may generalize by saying that Calderón's dazzlingly sure hand in dramatic construction and the troubling contradictions concerning values which his plays reveal are two sides of the same coin. The first provides at least a temporary release from the second, while the second provides argumental fuel for the first.

At the height of Calderón's Baroque dramaturgy, not only does art supply the spectator with precepts and doctrines but also with the artificial experiences against which he is to compare the general observation. We use the word "artificial" here because time and time again Calderón restructures his historical and mythical sources, as well as earlier plays, with the express purpose of illustrating a precept.[12] In accordance with the general Counter-Reformation concern with indoctrination, there is a constant preoccupation in Calderón's style that the abstract *moraleja* not be missed, a fear that, in Mateo Alemán's words, the audience may delight in the *conseja* and forget the *consejo*. To this end Calderón constructs obvious parallelisms, antinomies, extended metaphors, and didactic speeches, as if reason were in danger of coming to a conclusion that it should not draw and thus must be guided in a particular direction. His very insistence on certain verbal patterns and his use of certain stage techniques indicates that Calderón is not content with letting the dramatic story flow but must constantly call the audience's attention to the point that is being made. The fact that he found this conscious reiteration necessary reflects the uneasiness about values which constitutes the dominant note of so much of seventeenth-century Spanish culture.

These pragmatic and functional aspects of Calderonian dramaturgy have generally not been touched upon by the major currents of thought that have predominated in Calderón criticism since the 1940s, or at least they have been treated in a fashion quite different from that employed here. The innovative work of Parker, Dunn, Entwistle, Wardropper, May, and others has established the idea of a Calderonian world view. The theological, philosophical, poetic, and dramatic antecedents of Calderón have been systematically brought to light. Many plays and groups of plays have been set in a broader literary and ideological context. Yet, tacitly or explicitly, those critics approach the works of Calderón from the point of view of an ideology that tends to parallel the official doctrines of Calderón's age.[13] Their interest in Calderón may have been due in large part to an admiration and a sympathy with the world view contained in the *autos* and, by extension, in the *comedias.*[14]

We must go beyond the ethical and religious preoccupations that have guided much of the Anglo-German tradition of Calderón criticism. Critics of this tradition usually have an excellent technical grasp of medieval and Renaissance thought and art. However, they usually confine their critical tasks to expounding concepts such as "right reason" and "passions," and they do so in terms of categories that are themselves classical or Scholastic.

We have seen in the preceding chapters that in Calderón's *comedias,* "reason" in the singular does not exist, although many characters insist that it does. Likewise, "passions" are not merely a set of negative, passive responses that must be controlled by active reason, but rather they are creative forces. Although these notions do not receive a systematic verbal expression in Calderón, they were formulated clearly by later literature and philosophy.

The cracks which we have pointed out in what has generally been regarded as a rather solid Calderonian edifice may well turn out to be the most revealing elements of his drama. These cracks are seldom found at moments in which Calderón himself calls attention to a paradox or a dilemma. Rather, they are found in places which Calderón lets pass without comment. As modern readers, we can and should appreciate the profound irony of statements like the one from *Los cabellos de Absalón* which was quoted earlier: "Yo siempre la razón, señor, defiendo." The character who makes this statement has, like so many others, elevated his particular course of action and his particular loyalties into a participation in Reason itself. Recognizing the irony here in no way detracts from Calderón's greatness as a playwright nor does it prohibit us from calling him universally human. We may go so far as to say that Calderón's lasting aesthetic achievement in the *comedias* has not been his ingenuity in "dramatizing" or "illustrating" a coherent set of doctrines: in this respect, the *autos* perform the task much more economically. It is rather his representation, conscious or unconscious, of aristocratic figures in whom the rift between desires and obligations and between thought and action is vividly portrayed.

Thus this study has attempted to present Calderón's *comedias* in the light of the presupposition that the best way to appreciate his works is to acknowledge and understand the relativity of his stance as dramatist and ideologue. It is hoped that, as we enter the fourth century of Calderonian criticism, Calderón will be revalidated on different and more concretely historical bases.

Notes

Introduction

1 Max Kommerell describes Calderón's dramatic "ulterior motives" in the following terms: "Nie . . . ist die dramatische Form so sehr Vorwand für gewisse voraus entworfene Konfigurationen gewesen, nie hat sie so ausschliesslich dazu gedient, uns ein System der feinsten Bezüge vor die Sinne zu bringen, wie im Falle Calderóns, dessen gelungenste Szenen vom freien Geist des Spieles inspiriert sind"–*Beiträge zu einem deutschen Calderón* (Frankfurt-am-Main: Vittorio Klostermann, 1946), I, 164-65.

2 "Calderón, in his honor plays, describes the struggle of his characters for a false absolute, an absolute which is viewed by them as a horrible fatality, but in which Calderón himself does not believe and to which he opposes the Christian absolute"–Barbara K. Mujica, *Calderón's Don Lope de Almeida: A Kafkian Character* (New York: Plaza Mayor, 1971), p. 31.

3 T. E. May, although he still speaks in Scholastic terms, describes the difference in historical periods this way: "What generates the formal difference between [Calderón's] play and a medieval one is that Calderón has the great metaphysical passion of his times for the individual. . . . In Scholastic terms, haecceity is added to quiddity"–"The Symbolism of *El mágico prodigioso*," *Romanic Review,* 54 (1963), 96-97.

4 Two invaluable sources for a definition of the term "Baroque" as used in this study are: S. Gilman, "An Introduction to the Ideology of the Baroque in Spain," *Symposium,* 1 (1946), 82-107; Max Oppenheimer, "The Baroque Impasse in the Calderonian Drama," *PMLA,* 65 (1950), 1146-65.

5 James E. Maraniss, *On Calderón* (Columbia, Mo.: University of Missouri Press, 1978), p. 103. On the same page, he says in particular: "Parker . . . attributes his own morality to Calderón, which is a mistake."

6 Witness W. J. Entwistle's preference: "It was much better for Calderón when, in the *autos* of his last period, he was able to present his thoughts as a play of symbols only. It is hardly possible to avoid incongruence when making the abstract local and concrete"– "Justina's Temptation: An Approach to the Understanding of Calderón," *Modern Language Review,* 40 (July 1945), 189.

7 Perhaps the most extreme example of a critic who constructs a catalogue of concepts for interpretation of Calderón is Carlos Ortigoza Vieyra, whose work consists of listing a series of abstract *móviles* which enter into play in each scene of *El príncipe constante.* Cf. *Los móviles de la comedia* (Mexico: Robredo, 1957).

8 "[L']Espagne du XVIIe siècle adopte avec une extrême rigueur le rationalisme thomiste. Sa littérature ne peut se permettre le moindre écart par rapport à l'orthodoxie catholique"–Charles V. Aubrun, "Le Déterminisme naturel et la causalité surnaturelle chez Calderón," in *Le Théâtre tragique,* ed. Jean Jacquot, 2nd ed. (Paris: Centre National de la Recherche Scientifique, 1962), p. 199.

9 There is a study on Tirso de Molina which masterfully employs a living, dynamic reconstruction of Counter-Reformation intellectual life: Henry W. Sullivan, *Tirso de Molina and the Drama of the Counter Reformation* (Amsterdam: Rodopi, 1976).

10 A. A. Parker explicitly states why he holds this tenet: "The imagination, being unrestricted by historical convention, can clothe its fancies in any way it pleases"–*The Allegorical Drama of Calderón* (Oxford: Dolphin Book Co., 1943), p. 78.

11 Perhaps we should think of this Calderonian disorder as the exception that proves the rule: "Pero si, ante la constatación de que todo cambia, se juzga que todo en el mundo se encuentra tergiversado, es porque se piensa que existe una estructura racional por debajo, cuya alteración permite estimar la existencia de un desorden: si se puede hablar del mundo al revés es porque tiene un derecho"–José Antonio Maravall, *La cultura del barroco* (Esplugues de Llobregat: Ariel, 1975), p. 314.

12 Entwistle, "Justina's Temptation," pp. 180-89.

13 Benedetto Croce, *Letture di poeti* (Bari: Laterza, 1950), p. 24.

14 John V. Bryans, *Calderón de la Barca: Image, Drama and Rhetoric* (London: Tamesis, 1977), p. 67.

15 Bruce Wardropper, ed., *Teatro español del Siglo de Oro* (New York: Scribner's Sons, 1970), p. 677.

16 Robert D. F. Pring-Mill, "Estructuras lógico-retóricas y sus resonancias: un discurso de *El príncipe constante,*" in *Hacia Calderón II,* ed. Hans Flasche (Berlin: Walter de Gruyter, 1973), p. 113.

17 Bryans gives an admirably clear and thorough set of examples for each major rhetorical device.

18 Both authors quoted in Benedetto Croce, *Estetica come scienza dell' espressione,* 11th ed. (Bari: Laterza, 1965), p. 475.

19 Walter Benjamin, *The Origin of German Tragic Drama,* trans. John Osborne (London: NLB, 1977), p. 179.

20 José Antonio Maravall, "La función del honor en la sociedad tradicional," *Ideologies and Literature,* 2, No. 7 (May-June 1978), 13-14.

21 The protagonist stands out as an exemplary figure in Calderón more than in Lope: "Calderón's plays . . . show a clearer subordination of characters to the protagonist. Their parts are conceived in terms of his, their qualities and behaviour throw his into relief"

–A. E. Sloman, *The Dramatic Craftsmanship of Calderón: His Use of Earlier Plays* (Oxford: Dolphin Book Co., 1958), p. 294.

Chapter 1: The Thomistic Scheme of Reason and the Passions

1 H. D. Gardeil, O. P., *Introduction to the Philosophy of St. Thomas Aquinas* (St. Louis: Herder, 1956), III, 101-02.

2 John Beverley, "The Language of Contradiction: Aspects of Góngora's *Soledades,*" *Ideologies and Literature,* 1, No. 5 (Jan.-Feb. 1978), 30.

3 Aristotle, *De anima,* II, 2.

4 Cf. *Príncipe constante* (Act I): (description of breeze blowing through the flowers) "[Y] así al céfiro amoroso / matices rinde y olores, / que soplando en ellas bebe . . ." (Wardropper, ed., *Teatro español,* p. 617).

5 Gardeil, III, 66.

6 Pedro Calderón de la Barca, *Dramas de honor,* ed. Angel Valbuena Briones, 3rd ed., II (Madrid: Espasa-Calpe, 1970), 65. All quotes from *El médico* are from this edition, and henceforward only volume and page numbers will be cited in the text.

7 Real Academia Española, *Diccionario de Autoridades,* facsim. ed. (Madrid: Gredos, 1963), V, 615.

8 C. Plinius Secundus, *Natural History,* ed. H. Rackham (Cambridge, Mass.: Harvard University Press, 1940), III, 36.

9 "Analoge Namen sind solche, welche dieselbe Wortgestalt haben und verschiedene Begriffe bedeuten, deren Gegenstände aber in gewissen Beziehungen, in gewissen Proportionen, zueinander stehen"–Franz Manthey, *Die Sprachphilosophie des hl. Thomas von Aquin* (Paderborn: Verlag Ferdinand Schöningh, 1937), p. 121.

10 Angel L. Cilveti has this to say about such reasoning in Calderón: "La metáfora ayuda a llevar al espectador la convicción que el razonamiento no puede producir por sí solo porque es probable, no apodíctico. Esta insuficiencia demostrativa (en el orden silogístico de la identidad) alarga indefinidamente la cadena inductiva en busca de máxima probabilidad, a base de una diseminación metafórica"–"Silogismo, correlación e imagen poética en el teatro de Calderón," *Romanische Forschungen,* 80, No. 4 (1968), 494-95.

11 "Für die Logik ist wichtig, dass äquivoken Namen als *signa ambigua* leicht Anlass von Täuschungen und Trugschlüssen werden können, heisst doch ein Trugschluss *fallacia aequivocationis*" (Manthey, p. 120).

12 Luis de Góngora y Argote, *Obras completas,* ed. Juan Millé y Giménez and Isabel Millé y Giménez, 5th ed. (Madrid: Aguilar, 1961), p. 445.

13 Plinius Secundus, X, 210.

14 Gardeil, III, 76-78.

15 Suárez calls the *aestimativa* a "[s]ensus interior potens apprehendere sub ratione convenientis vel disconvenientis, seu sub ratione insensata"–quoted in Salvador Castellote Cubells, *Die Anthropologie des Suárez* (Munich: Verlag K. A. Freiburg, 1962), p. 143.

16 Aristotle, *On the Soul,* trans. W. S. Hett (London: Heinemann, 1957), p. 179. The mind assumes the form, that is, becomes identical with its object, but not in the sense in which matter receives a form to become an existing substance.

17 Gardeil, III, 162.

18 *Summa Theologiae,* Ia, qu. 85, art. 5.

19 Etienne Gilson, *Le Thomisme,* 5th ed. (Paris: J. Vrin, 1947), p. 332.

20 Ernst Cassirer, *The Individual and the Cosmos in Renaissance Philosophy,* trans. Mario Domandi (New York: Barnes and Noble, 1963), p. 84.

21 This expression, of course, is not peculiar to Calderón, but is found in the writings of a great number of Spanish seventeenth-century authors. Leo Spitzer has studied the phrase thoroughly and has related it to the *sum qui sum* which Jehovah pronounces to Moses in the Vulgate Old Testament. He notes, however, that the following distinction must always be made between the manifestation of the divine essence and of the human: "Siempre habrá la enorme diferencia de que el ser humano que 'es el que es' se orienta de acuerdo con su pasado (o con el de su familia), mientras que Dios se sitúa fuera del tiempo, y de que, por otra parte, el ser humano debe ver una obligación en el mantenimiento de su continuidad, en tanto que Dios es lo que es por su naturaleza perfecta"– Leo Spitzer, *"Soy quien soy," Nueva Revista de Filología Hispánica,* 1 (1947), 125.

22 *Summa Theologiae,* IaIIae, qu. 22-30.

23 It will readily be seen that the eleven basic emotions described above are differentiated from one another according to three criteria: (1) whether their object is a good or an evil, (2) whether they constitute a movement toward or a movement away from the object, and (3) whether the object's attainment or avoidance is direct or involves difficulty. These are called specific differences because they classify the passions into different species.

24 Pedro Calderón de la Barca, *El mayor monstro los çelos,* ed. Everett W. Hesse (Madison: University of Wisconsin Press, 1955), p. 92. All quotes of this *comedia* are from this edition, and henceforward only page numbers will be cited in the text.

25 This concept is sometimes translated into a social metaphor. Balbino Marcos Villanueva points out in Calderón's *El año santo de Roma* the idea of the soul as an "espíritu noble" that governs the body, which is a "rústico villano"–*La ascética de los jesuitas en los autos sacramentales de Calderón* (Bilbao: Universidad de Deusto, 1973), pp. 180-81.

26 Gilson, *Le Thomisme*, pp. 338-39.

27 F. H. Sandbach, *The Stoics* (London: Chatto and Windus, 1975), p. 17.

28 Pedro Calderón de la Barca, *Comedias religiosas*, ed. Angel Valbuena Briones, 3rd ed. (Madrid: Espasa-Calpe, 1946), I, 201. All quotes from *El mágico* are from this edition, and henceforward only volume and page numbers will be cited in the text.

29 Marcus Aurelius Antoninus, *Communings With Himself*, trans. C. R. Haines (London: William Heinemann, 1916), p. 49. All quotes from this work are from this editon, and henceforward only page numbers will be cited in the text.

30 Walter Benjamin remarks in relation to this passage: "Even in their isolation the words reveal themselves as fateful. Indeed, one is tempted to say that the very fact that they still have a meaning in their isolation lends a threatening quality to this remnant of meaning they have kept. In this way language is broken up so as to acquire a changed and intensified meaning in its fragments" (p. 208).

31 Gardeil, III, 202-05.

32 In Suárez' words, "intellectus tantum potest movere finaliter voluntatem, voluntas vero intellectum effective"–Francisco Suárez, *De anima*, in *Opera omnia*, ed. D. M. André (Paris: "Luis Vives," 1856), III, 773.

33 "[V]oluntas consequitur intellectum: ergo ejus actus eo se extendit, quo apprehensio intellectus: sed hic potest apprehendere omne bonum: ergo et voluntas ipsum prosequi" (Suárez, *De anima*, III, 771).

34 Again, in Suárez' words, "prius, ac perfectius moralis bonitas oritur ab intellectu, qua de causa etiam dependentia, quae inter virtutes morales perfectissima est, in intellectu residet" (Suárez, *De anima*, III, 777).

35 "Towards a Definition of Calderonian Tragedy," *Bulletin of Hispanic Studies*, 39 (1962), 222-37.

Chapter 2: Matrimonial Plays

1 I am referring here to two studies in particular: P. N. Dunn, "Honor and the Christian Background," *Bulletin of Hispanic Studies*, 37 (April 1960), 75-105; Bruce Wardropper, "Poesía y drama en *El médico de su honra* de Calderón," trans. O. Durán D'Ocón, in *Calderón y la crítica*, ed. Durán and González Echevarría (Madrid: Gredos, 1976), II, 582-97.

2 This overweening concern contradicts the principle in Thomism that one's being (*esse*) determines how one is related to others. For Gilson, Thomistic philosophy "est empruntée tout entière aux divers aspects d'une même idée, l'idée d'être. La pensée humaine ne se satisfait que lorsqu'elle s'empare d'une existence" (*Le Thomisme*, p. 497).

3 *Summa Theologiae*, IIaIIae, qu. 103, art. 1.

4 St. Thomas Aquinas, *Summa Theologiae* (London: Blackfriars, 1964-74), XLI, 117. All direct quotes from the *Summa* are from the Blackfriars editions, and henceforward only volume and page numbers will be cited in the text.

5 Pedro Calderón de la Barca, *Dramas de honor*, ed. Angel Valbuena Briones, I (Madrid: Espasa-Calpe, 1967), 65. All quotes from *A secreto agravio* are from this edition, and henceforward only volume and page numbers will be cited in the text.

6 *A secreto agravio*, Act III:

> DON LOPE: ¿En qué tribunal se ha visto
> condenar al inocente?
> ¿Sentencias hay sin delito?
> ¿Informaciones sin cargo?
> Y sin culpas ¿hay castigo?
>
>   (I, 74-75)

7 Rabelais captures the ideal of the medieval truthseeker (albeit satirically) in his Thaumaste: "Seigneur, aultre chose ne m'ameine, sinon bon désir de apprendre et sçavoir ce dont j'ay doubté toute ma vie. . . . Et au regard de disputer par contention, je ne le veulx faire; aussi est-ce chose trop vile, et la laisse à ces maraulx de Sophistes"—François Rabelais, *Pantagruel*, ed. V. L. Saulnier (Geneva: Droz, 1965), p. 108.

8 "Next to sadness, fear best reveals the characteristics of passion, because it is eminently passive; and the organic disturbances which it produces are most apparent"—Etienne Gilson, *The Christian Philosophy of St. Thomas Aquinas*, trans. L. K. Shook (New York: Random House, 1956), p. 284.

9 "The judge's duty, to be sure, is to chastise the guilty, and all of us must condemn the wicked in our inner forum. But it is better to err many times by acquitting the guilty than even rarely to condemn the innocent" (Gilson, *The Christian Philosophy*, p. 311).

10 Wardropper, "Poesía y drama," passim.

11 Cf. E. M. Wilson, "La discreción de don Lope de Almeida," *Clavileño*, 2, No. 9 (June 1951), 1-10.

12 Aristotle, *On Interpretation. Commentary by St. Thomas and Cajetan*, trans. Jean T. Oesterle (Milwaukee: Marquette University Press, 1962), p. 23.

13 Aristotle, *On Interpretation*, p. 28.

14 Ancius Manlius Severinus Boetius, *Commentarii in librum Aristotelis Peri hermeneias*, ed. Karl Meiser (Leipzig: Teubner, 1877), I, 37.

15 Wardropper ("Poesía y drama") develops this point extensively.

16 *Diccionario de Autoridades*, VI, 566.

17 This is made difficult by the dual nature of language: "Calderón se encuentra prontamente con las dos caras de la palabra, la que precisa y la que confunde. Esta es la causa

por la que, acogiéndose al espíritu de la época, se ayuda de la rigurosa arquitectura de la Escolástica"—Angel Valbuena Briones, *Ensayo sobre la obra de Calderón* (Madrid: Ateneo, 1958), p. 9.

18 *Siete Partidas,* II, XIII, 4. Quoted in Luciana de Stéfano, *La sociedad estamental de la Baja Edad Media española a la luz de la literatura de la época* (Caracas: Universidad Central de Venezuela, 1966), p. 109.

19 A good example would be Ferrand Mexía, *Nobiliario vero* (1492), in which the doctrine of nobility by lineage is defended with quotes and examples from the Bible, classical poets, and Fathers of the Church.

20 Antonio Domínguez Ortiz, *Las clases privilegiadas en la España del Antiguo Regimen* (Madrid: ISTMO, 1973), p. 186.

21 Quoted in Domínguez Ortiz, p. 188.

22 TETRARCA: "[Y] el mío es tan grande, / que pienso (atiende Filipo) / que pasando los vmbrales / de la muerte, a de quedar / a las futuras edades / grabado con letras de oro / en láminas de diamante" (p. 52).

23 Everett Hesse seems to sympathize with Herodes' reasoning: "Calderón, by associating the conduct of Herod with that of all lovers and husbands who would rather see their sweethearts or wives dead than in the arms of another, thus strikes a note of appeal which strengthens his point of contact with the audience, who can better understand the Tetrarch's feelings . . ." (Introd., *El mayor monstro los çelos,* p. 26).

24 "Parto u producción contra el orden regular de la naturaleza" (*Diccionario de Autoridades,* IV, 598).

25 ". . . *El major munstro del mondo* [sic] has been described as the first drama of fate in world literature" (Benjamin, pp. 83-84).

Chapter 3: Political Plays

1 John Dowling, *Diego de Saavedra Fajardo* (Boston: Twayne, 1977), pp. 62-63.

2 Dowling, p. 69.

3 Baltasar Gracián, *El héroe,* ed. Adolphe Coster (Chartres: Librairie Lester, 1911), p. 9. All quotes from *El héroe* are from this edition, and henceforward only page numbers will be cited in the text.

4 Eugenio Frutos Cortés finds this distinction made in some of Calderón's *autos:* "[E]l Ingenio no es la simple intelección pura, sino la facultad de *inventar* (de intuir, acaso, pudiéramos decir hoy), mientras el Entendimiento es la facultad de *elegir* o discernir (esto es, de juzgar)"—*La filosofía de Calderón en sus autos sacramentales* (Zaragoza: Institución "Fernando el Católico," 1952), p. 153.

5 Baltasar Gracián, *El político*, ed. E. Tierno Galván (Salamanca: Anaya, 1961), p. 46.

6 Francisco de Quevedo, *Política de Dios*, ed. James O. Crosby (Madrid: Castalia, 1966), p. 38. All quotes from this work are from this edition, and henceforward only page numbers will be cited in the text.

7 "[S]i en algunos casos se escucha el eco arcaizante del tema medieval y ascético del 'de contemptu mundi' como preparación a una disciplina religiosa, en el siglo barroco se observa comúnmente en la materia un considerable grado de secularización que hace que de la práctica de la desconfianza ante el mundo y el hombre, todos procuren sacar las convenientes artes para vencerlos en provecho propio" (Maravall, *La cultura*, p. 327).

8 Dowling, pp. 101-02.

9 In the following section, I am heavily indebted to José Antonio Maravall, *Teoría española del estado en el siglo XVII* (Madrid: Instituto de Estudios Políticos, 1944), pp. 229-72.

10 Quoted in *Summa Theologiae*, XXXVI, 82.

11 Maravall, *Teoría española*, p. 237.

12 Diego Saavedra Fajardo, *Empresas políticas: Idea de un príncipe político-cristiano*, ed. Quintín Aldea Vaquero (Madrid: Editora Nacional, 1976), I, 121. All quotes from the *Empresas* are from this edition, and henceforward only volume and page numbers will be cited in the text.

13 Maravall, *Teoría española*, p. 234.

14 Pedro Calderón de la Barca, *Primera parte de comedias*, ed. Angel Valbuena Briones (Madrid: Consejo Superior de Investigaciones Científicas, 1974), I, 4. All quotes from *La gran Cenobia* are from this edition, and henceforward only volume and page numbers will be cited in the text.

15 Cf. T. E. May, "Segismundo y el soldado rebelde," in *Hacia Calderón I* (Berlin: Walter de Gruyter, 1970), pp. 71-76.

16 He performs a work of self-realization: "El hombre realiza sobre sí mismo y sobre los demás un trabajo de alfarero. Esto es lo que representa una obra como la de Gracián y en ella su más radical significación: el paso de una moral a una moralística, o digamos simplemente a una reflexión sobre la práctica de la conducta que . . . podemos llamar un 'arte de la conducta'—dando a la palabra *arte* su valor de una *técnica*" (Maravall, *La cultura*, p. 346).

17 "Calderón constructs his plays to emphasize the will, which, no matter how powerful the obstacles to its functioning, always functions and always succeeds" (Maraniss, p. 14).

18 Alan Paterson, "The Traffic of the Stage in Calderón's *La vida es sueño*," *Renaissance Drama*, 1971, p. 180.

19 Barry W. Ife, "Castigos y premios en *La vida es sueño*," in *Hacia Calderón III*, ed. Hans Flasche (Berlin: Walter de Gruyter, 1976), p. 32.

20 Ife, p. 43.

21 Pedro Calderón de la Barca, *La vida es sueño y El alcalde de Zalamea*, ed. Augusto Cortina, 4th ed. (Madrid: Espasa-Calpe, 1968), p. 110.

22 T. E. May, "Segismundo," p. 74.

23 Gwynne Edwards, Introd., *Los cabellos de Absalón*, by Pedro Calderón (Oxford: Pergamon Press, 1973), pp. 1-33.

24 Edwards, p. 16.

25 H. F. Giacoman sees David as quite the opposite: "David es el encargado de enunciar la posición cristiana de la Iglesia católica. Es el campeón del libre albedrío"–*Estudio y edición crítica de la comedia "Los cabellos de Absalón"* (University of North Carolina: Estudios de Hispanófila, 1968), p. 50.

26 *Los cabellos*, ed. Edwards, p. 127. Henceforward only page numbers will be cited in the text.

27 Actually, this speech, like all of Act II of *Los cabellos*, is virtually lifted from Tirso de Molina, but following Edwards' interpretation of the problem, I assume here that at least the general lines of the act, including the metaphors, are in line with Calderón's dramatic purpose (Edwards, p. 14).

Chapter 4: Philosophical Plays

1 Góngora, *Obras completas*, p. 659.

2 Sor Juana Inés de la Cruz, *Obras escogidas* (Madrid: Espasa-Calpe, 1969), p. 45.

3 Cf. Cervantes' treatment of the debate in *Don Quijote*, I, Chap. 38.

4 Pedro Calderón de la Barca, *La estatua de Prometeo*, ed. Charles V. Aubrun (Paris: Centre de Recherches de l'Institut d'Etudes Hispaniques, 1965), p. 5. All quotes of the play are from this edition, and henceforward only page numbers will be cited in the text.

5 Giovanni Boccaccio, *Genealogia Deorum Gentilium Libri* (Bari: Laterza, 1951), I, 199.

6 *Summa Theologiae*, IIaIIae, qu. 182, art. 1. Charles Aubrun accepts this Thomistic concept: "Les Lettres discrètement l'emportent sur les Armes. Et sur le monde rasséréné triomphent la Raison et la Paix" (Pref., *La estatua*, p. xxix).

7 Angel Valbuena Briones, *Perspectiva crítica de los dramas de Calderón* (Madrid: Rialp, 1965), p. 397.

8 Such is the base on which rests Maurice Scève's Platonic poem cycle *Délie, Object de Plus Haulte Vertu*. The lady's name can be taken as an anagram for *l'Idée*.

9 Don William Cruickshank, Introd., *En la vida todo es verdad y todo mentira*, by Pedro Calderón de la Barca (London: Tamesis, 1971), p. cxxvi.

10 Cruickshank, p. c.

11 *En la vida*, ed. Cruickshank, p. 74. All quotes from this play are from the Cruickshank edition, and henceforward only page numbers will be cited in the text.

12 Cruickshank, p. cx.

13 Cruickshank, p. cxxviii.

14 In the Baroque age, "[l]a imagen senequista del sabio que se juzga libre en su reflexión interna, incluso tras la reja de una cárcel, queda . . . eliminada" (Maravall, *La cultura*, p. 350).

15 "A la primera ojeada, el raciocinio de Calderón parece poseer el aspecto de una busca sin fin de la verdad nueva; pero un escrutinio más detallado muestra que es siempre una verdad, que, en efecto, en su filosofía se considera como fija y completa por toda la eternidad. El método dialéctico no es nada investigatorio; es un invento de Aristóteles, que en el teatro de Calderón extrae las consecuencias de las verdades ya conocidas por la enseñanza de la Iglesia, más bien que buscar verdades nuevas"–Everett Hesse, "La dialéctica y el casuismo en Calderón," in *Calderón y la crítica*, ed. Durán and González Echevarría (Madrid: Gredos, 1976), II, 580-81.

Chapter 5: *Comedias de santos*

1 To a certain extent, A. A. Parker does this by subordinating the plot to the moral or theological theme.

2 Hugo Friedrich sees immanent laws rather than an extrinsic God as the source of moral judgements in the secular plays: "Gott greift nicht persönlich ein. Die über dem Menschen herrschenden Gesetze, so wie Calderón sie sieht, sprechen sich im Lebensstoff selber aus, in symbolischer Allgültigkeit: die schuldhafte Verführung durch Macht und Schönheit,–die Unentrinnbarkeit des Geschicks, sobald der Mensch auf Erden gerufen ist, –die ergreifbare oder verfehlbare Freiheit, selbst im Unentrinnbarkeit das optimal Rechte zu tun,–und schliesslich die Vergeblichkeit von Macht und Schönheit"–*Der fremde Calderón* (Freiburg: H. F. Schulz Verlag, 1955), pp. 38-39.

3 Valbuena Briones discovers a humorous element in the Devil's intervention: "El Demonio tiene todas las posibilidades y recursos de un teatro ejemplar. Puebla la imaginación de fantasmas, da apariencia de lo que no es, paraliza el curso normal de los acontecimientos, que quedan en suspensión, y un espíritu de burla se enseñorea momentáneamente de las situaciones" (*Ensayo*, p. 40).

4 Calderón, *Obras completas*, 5th ed. (Madrid: Aguilar, 1969), I, 668. All quotes from

Las cadenas are from this edition, and henceforward only volume and page numbers will be cited in the text.

5 "[F]or the theatre of profane society . . . the power of salvation and redemption only ever lies in a paradoxical reflection of play and appearance. In the ideal romantic *Trauerspiel* of Calderón the mourning [*Trauer*] is dispersed by that intentionality which, according to Goethe, emanates from every work of art. The new theatre has artifice as its god" (Benjamin, p. 82).

6 A. A. Parker, "The Devil in the Drama of Calderón," in *Critical Essays on the Theatre of Calderón,* ed. Bruce Wardropper (New York: New York University Press, 1965), pp. 4-5.

7 T. E. May, "The Symbolism," pp. 110-11.

8 Parker ("The Devil," p. 16) notes that this fact might "provoke the cynical comment that medieval men portrayed the Devil as being more honest than themselves." Why cynical?

9 Parker, "The Devil," p. 20.

10 Benjamin reminds us that "it will never be true that the task of the dramatist is to exhibit the causal necessity of a sequence of events on the stage. Why should art reinforce a thesis which it is the business of deterministic philosophy to advance?" (p. 129).

11 A. E. Sloman does not share the point of view expressed here: "Every action in Calderón's plays is motivated" (p. 286).

12 "Cipriano is a man who has blundered into a cosmic struggle he does not understand" (T. E. May, "The Symbolism," p. 101).

13 "Dass die Naturstimmen ebensogut ein Echo der Gefühle Justinas sind, als sie diese Gefühle erregen, ist so ausgesprochen; die Szene lässt sich sowohl altertümlich als modern-subjektiv auffassen" (Kommerell, I, 79).

14 This analogy can be made in a certain sense for the entire Counter-Reformation movement: "[I]f the Counter Reformation repudiated revolutionary ideas in its official thinking, it assimilated the force of Renaissance attitudes in its behavior. The sheer energy and corporate enterprise, the business and aspiration that went into the Catholic revival are clearly of their age. The fundamental paradox of the campaign lay in the practical attempts of 'modern' men to reimpose theoretical medieval standards; to act intuitively in heart and limb in ways which the head had in principle ruled arrogant and anti-authoritarian" (Sullivan, p. 27).

15 According to Entwistle, "[t]he conclusions of *El mágico prodigioso* hold, because they are dogmatic; the premisses employed are also true, since they are dogmas, and not merely parts of an apparently valid demonstration" ("Justina's Temptation," p. 187).

Chapter 6: Conclusion

1 "Predomina . . . en Calderón la tradición medieval de la Escolástica sobre el rena-centismo, pues reivindica al hombre por razones sobrenaturales y no por excelencias de su propia naturaleza" (Frutos Cortés, p. 211).

2 Max Oppenheimer believes that also the meaning of the word *albedrío* has shifted accordingly: "Thus, in Calderón, the word *albedrío*, besides being used in matters pertaining to religious choice, often refers to man's power to decide on his own course of action, to do as he wills, without having to yield to the deterministic forces of destiny and nature or the commands of society and individuals" (pp. 1146-65).

3 "La foi est implorée pour apaiser la tempête, la raison est mobilisée pour servir la croyance, mais toute idéologie n'est qu'un effort de conjurer des forces irrationnelles par des suggestions irrationnelles"–Anton L. Constandse, *Le Baroque espagnol et Calderón de la Barca* (Amsterdam: Boekhandel "Plus Ultra," 1951), p. 131.

4 "Many passages in Calderón clearly refer to, or imply, the fact that the characters still look upon reason as a panacea and the only means by which man can prevent error, solve human problems, and realize self. Reason, of course, proves an entirely inadequate tool for such purposes . . ." (Oppenheimer, p. 1153).

5 Karl Mannheim mentions "Machiavelli as one of the first writers to analyze events in the highest strata of society in terms of a mundane power process, stripped of their metaphysical aura of mystery"–*Essays on the Sociology of Culture* (London: Routledge and Kegan Paul, 1956), p. 214.

6 Jaime Vicéns Vives, *Approaches to the History of Spain* (Berkeley: University of California Press, 1967), p. 105.

7 See Beverley, pp. 28-56.

8 On the other hand, John V. Bryans feels that Calderón's edifice was sturdy enough: "In Calderón's language, the disorder of the world is clearly reflected, as are the reasons why it can never fully be vanquished; yet, at least within his plays, that language is one of the most important means by which he produces an order sufficiently subtle and complex to withstand and contain the forces of chaos" (p. 187).

9 "Every work of art has an indivisible twofold character: it expresses reality but also forms it"–Karel Kosík, *Dialectics of the Concrete* (Dordrecht: D. Reidel, 1976), p. 71.

10 "The 're-feudalization' of European society during the sixteenth and seventeenth centuries by no means restored early medieval feudalism; it rather combined feudal elements with novel forms of stratification and novel techniques of control. . . . What the new age did was to neutralize the effects of the earlier conquests of the *Ratio*, by blunting its cutting edge where it could be a menace to the new absolute authority" (Mannheim, p. 224).

11 "Là où il risque de quitter le terrain éclairé par la foi il s'arrête, et les instruments dont il se sert pour se construire le grillage qui borne le domaine de sa limitation volontaire sont les paroles qui forment le treillis de sa verbosité" (Constandse, p. 66).

12 Sloman (p. 296) sees this procedure as justified by Calderón's thematic purpose: "Calderón's search for a significant theme and his insistence that each character should fit into a thematic pattern necessitated often the distortion of history or legend."

13 See, for instance, Charles Aubrun's statement concerning his approach to *La estatua de Prometeo*: "Nous adoptons la méthode de critique des textes en vigueur au XVIIe siècle. On en cherchera les règles dans la *Philosophia secreta* de Pérez de Moya, qui les reprend de Léon Hébreu" (Pref., *La estatua*, p. xv, note 1).

14 "[Calderón] penetrated beneath the multifarious and seemingly capricious incidents of the stories of the sources to an underlying idea of universal application" (Sloman, p. 308).

Works Consulted

I. Lexical Source

Real Academia Española. *Diccionario de Autoridades.* 6 vols. 1726; facsim. ed. Madrid: Gredos, 1963.

II. Theological, Philosophical, and Philological Sources

Aquinas, Saint Thomas. *Summa Theologiae.* 60 vols. London: Blackfriars, 1964-74.

Aristotle. *On the Soul.* Trans. W. S. Hett. London: Heinemann, 1957.

———. *On Interpretation. Commentary by St. Thomas and Cajetan.* Trans. and ed. Jean T. Oesterle. Milwaukee: Marquette University Press, 1962.

Aurelius Antoninus, Marcus. *Communings With Himself.* Trans. C. R. Haines. London: Heinemann, 1916.

Boccaccio, Giovanni. *Genealogia Deorum Gentilium Libri.* Ed. Vincenzo Romano. 2 vols. Bari: Laterza, 1951.

Boetius, Ancius Manlius Severinus. *Commentarii in librum Aristotelis Peri hermeneias.* Ed. Karl Meiser. 2 vols. Leipzig: Teubner, 1877.

———. *De consolatione philosophiae.* London: Burns Oates and Washbourne, 1925.

Cassirer, Ernst. *The Individual and the Cosmos in Renaissance Philosophy.* Trans. Mario Domandi. New York: Barnes and Noble, 1963.

Castellote Cubells, Salvador. *Die Anthropologie des Suárez.* Munich: Verlag Karl Alber Freiburg, 1962.

Epictetus. *Encheiridion.* Ed. Charles Thurot. Paris: Hachette, 1874.

Gardeil, H. D. *Introduction to the Philosophy of St. Thomas Aquinas.* St. Louis: Herder, 1956. Vol. III.

Gilson, Etienne. *The Christian Philosophy of St. Thomas Aquinas.* Trans. L. K. Shook. New York: Random House, 1956.

———. *Le Thomisme.* 5th ed. Paris: J. Vrin, 1947.

Gracián, Baltasar. *El héroe.* Ed. Adolphe Coster. Chartres: Librairie Lester, 1911.

———. *El político.* Ed. E. Tierno Galván. Salamanca: Anaya, 1961.

Kosík, Karel. *Dialectics of the Concrete.* Dordrecht: D. Reidel, 1976.

Manthey, Franz. *Die Sprachphilosophie des hl. Thomas von Aquin.* Paderborn: Verlag Ferdinand Schöningh, 1937.

Marcos Villanueva, Balbino. *La ascética de los jesuitas en los autos sacramentales de Calderón.* Bilbao: Universidad de Deusto, 1973.

Plinius Secundus, C. *Natural History.* Ed. H. Rackham. 10 vols. Cambridge, Mass.: Harvard University Press, 1940.

Quevedo, Francisco de. *Política de Dios.* Ed. James O. Crosby. Madrid: Castalia, 1966.

Saavedra Fajardo, Diego. *Empresas políticas: Idea de un príncipe político-cristiano.* Ed. Quintín Aldea Vaquero. 2 vols. Madrid: Editora Nacional, 1976.

Sandbach, F. H. *The Stoics.* London: Chatto and Windus, 1975.

Spinoza, Benedict de. *Ethics.* Ed. James Gutman. New York: Harper, 1949.

Suárez, Francisco. *De anima.* In *Opera omnia.* Ed. D. M. André. Paris: "Luis Vives," 1856. Vol. III.

III. Historical Background Sources

Domínguez Ortiz, Antonio. *Las clases privilegiadas en la España del Antiguo Regimen.* Madrid: ISTMO, 1973.

———. *The Golden Age of Spain: 1516-1659.* Trans. James Casey. New York: Basic Books, 1971.

Lynch, John. *Spain Under the Hapsburgs.* 2 vols. Oxford: Basil Blackwell, 1969.

Mannheim, Karl. *Essays on the Sociology of Culture.* London: Routledge and Kegan Paul, 1956.

Maravall, José Antonio. *La cultura del barroco.* Esplugues de Llobregat: Ariel, 1975.

———. *La teoría española del estado en el siglo XVII.* Madrid: Instituto de Estudios Políticos, 1944.

Vicéns Vives, Jaime. *Approaches to the History of Spain*. Berkeley: University of California Press, 1967.

IV. Literary Background Sources

Benjamin, Walter. *The Origin of German Tragic Drama*. Trans. John Osbourne. London: NLB, 1977.

Beverley, John. "The Language of Contradiction: Aspects of Góngora's *Soledades*." *Ideologies and Literature*, 1, No. 5 (Jan.-Feb. 1978), 28-56.

Croce, Benedetto. *Estetica come scienza dell' espressione*. 11th ed. Bari: Laterza, 1965.

———. *Letture di poeti*. Bari: Laterza, 1950.

Cruz, Sor Juana Inés de la. *Obras escogidas*. 13th ed. Madrid: Espasa-Calpe, 1969.

Dowling, John. *Diego de Saavedra Fajardo*. Boston: Twayne, 1977.

Góngora y Argote, Luis de. *Obras completas*. Ed. Juan Millé y Giménez and Isabel Millé y Giménez. 5th ed. Madrid: Aguilar, 1961.

Spitzer, Leo. "*Soy quien soy*." *Nueva Revista de Filología Hispánica*, 1 (1947), 113-27.

Sullivan, Henry W. *Tirso de Molina and the Drama of the Counter Reformation*. Amsterdam: Rodopi, 1976.

V. Selected General Works on Calderón

Aubrun, Charles V. "Le Déterminisme naturel et la causalité surnaturelle chez Calderón." In *Le Théâtre tragique*. Ed. Jean Jacquot. 2nd ed. Paris: Centre National de la Recherche Scientifique, 1962.

Bryans, John V. *Calderón de la Barca: Imagery, Drama and Rhetoric*. London: Tamesis, 1977.

Cilveti, Angel L. "Silogismo, correlación e imagen poética en el teatro de Calderón." *Romanische Forschungen*, 80, No. 4 (1968), 459-97.

Constandse, Anton L. *Le Baroque espagnol et Calderón de la Barca*. Amsterdam: Boekhandel "Plus Ultra," 1951.

Dunn, P. N. "Honor and the Christian Background." *Bulletin of Hispanic Studies*, 37, No. 2 (April 1960), 75-105.

Friedrich, Hugo. *Der fremde Calderón*. Freiburg: H. F. Schulz Verlag, 1955.

Frutos Cortés, Eugenio. *La filosofía de Calderón en sus autos sacramentales.* Zaragoza: Institución "Fernando el Católico," 1952.

Hesse, Everett W. *Calderón de la Barca.* New York: Twayne, 1967.

————. "La dialéctica y el casuismo en Calderón." In *Calderón y la crítica.* Ed. Manuel Durán and Roberto González Echevarría. Madrid: Gredos, 1976, II, 563-81.

Kommerell, Max. *Beiträge zu einem deutschen Calderón.* 2 vols. Frankfurt: Vittorio Klostermann, 1946.

Maraniss, James E. *On Calderón.* Columbia, Mo.: University of Missouri Press, 1978.

Oppenheimer, Max. "The Baroque Impasse in the Calderonian Drama." *PMLA,* 65 (1950), 1146-65.

Ortigoza Vieyra, Carlos. *Los móviles de la comedia.* Mexico: Robredo, 1957.

Parker, A. A. *The Allegorical Drama of Calderón.* Oxford: Dolphin Book Co., 1943.

————. "The Devil in the Drama of Calderón." In *Critical Essays on the Theatre of Calderón.* Ed. Bruce Wardropper. New York: New York University Press, 1965, pp. 3-23.

————. "Towards a Definition of Calderonian Tragedy." *Bulletin of Hispanic Studies,* 39 (1962), 222-37.

Sloman, A. E. *The Dramatic Craftsmanship of Calderón: His Use of Earlier Plays.* Oxford: Dolphin Book Co., 1958.

Valbuena Briones, Angel. *Ensayo sobre la obra de Calderón.* Madrid: Ateneo, 1958.

————. *Perspectiva crítica de los dramas de Calderón.* Madrid: Rialp, 1965.

Valbuena Prat, Angel, introd. *Comedias religiosas.* By Pedro Calderón de la Barca. Madrid: Espasa-Calpe, 1930, I, 9-65.

VI. Selected Studies on Individual *Comedias*

Aubrun, Charles V., introd. *La estatua de Prometeo.* By Pedro Calderón de la Barca. Paris: Centre de Recherches de l'Institut d'Etudes Hispaniques, 1965.

Blue, William R. "¿Qué es esto que miro?: Converging Sign Systems in *El médico de su honra." Bulletin of Comediantes,* 30 (1978), 83-96.

Cruickshank, Don William, introd. *En la vida todo es verdad y todo mentira.* By Pedro Calderón de la Barca. London: Tamesis, 1971, pp. xi-cxxxiii.

Edwards, Gwynne, introd. *Los cabellos de Absalón*. By Pedro Calderón de la Barca. Oxford: Pergamon Press, 1973, pp. 1-33.

Entwistle, W. J. "Justina's Temptation: An Approach to the Understanding of Calderón." *Modern Language Review*, 40 (July 1945), 180-89.

Giacoman, Helmy Fuad. *Estudio y edición crítica de la comedia "Los cabellos de Absalón."* University of North Carolina: Estudios de Hispanófila, 1968.

Hesse, Everett W., introd. *El mayor monstro los çelos*. By Pedro Calderón de la Barca. Madison: University of Wisconsin Press, 1955, pp. 1-35.

Ife, Barry W. "Castigos y premios en *La vida es sueño*." In *Hacia Calderón III*. Ed. Hans Flasche. Berlin: Walter de Gruyter, 1976, pp. 32-46.

May, T. E. "Segismundo y el soldado rebelde." In *Hacia Calderón I*. Ed. A. A. Parker and Hans Flasche. Berlin: Walter de Gruyter, 1970, pp. 71-76.

———. "The Symbolism of *El mágico prodigioso*." *Romanic Review*, 54 (1963), 93-112.

Mujica, Barbara Kaminar de. *Calderón's Don Lope de Almeida: A Kafkian Character*. New York: Plaza Mayor, 1971.

Paterson, Alan. "The Traffic of the Stage in Calderón's *La vida es sueño*." *Renaissance Drama*, 1971, pp. 155-83.

Pring-Mill, Robert D. F. "Estructuras lógico-retóricas y sus resonancias: un discurso de *El príncipe constante*." In *Hacia Calderón II*. Ed. Hans Flasche. Berlin: Walter de Gruyter, 1973, pp. 109-54.

Wardropper, Bruce. "The Interplay of Wisdom and Saintliness in *El mágico prodigioso*." *Hispanic Review*, 11 (1943), 116-24.

———. "Poesía y drama en *El médico de su honra* de Calderón." Trans. O. Durán D'Ocón. In *Calderón y la crítica*. Ed. Manuel Durán and Robert González Echevarría. Madrid: Gredos, 1976, II, 582-97.

Wilson, E. M. "La discreción de don Lope de Almeida." *Clavileño*, 2, No. 9 (June 1951), 1-10.